100+ Recipes that Work

To Tracy & Bailey,

"Never Eat Alone"

William Kennedy

Published By William Kennedy
Franklin, TN 37064

ISBN: 978-0-615-18271-1

Printed & Bound in U.S.A

Introduction

Learning to cook is easier than knowing what to cook. It may not appear so; hence my book - 100+ Recipes that work. Like all guys and some gals, I never gave cooking a thought. While growing up, meals were made by Mom, or perhaps by a neighbor or a relative. Sometimes a group effort, civic or church related, was the provider. Then came college or the military service. Again, meals were provided.

Marriage came after 2 years of this bachelor life. My wife was and is an excellent cook. We are married almost as long as Moses spent wandering in the desert. I am retired now for the 2nd Time. In my "idle" moments a thought came to me. Learn to cook. I did. It is great fun and Wow! It turned out well. After about 8 years, I can say it is terrific.

You could find better recipes and easier preparations. Nevertheless, the recipes in this book are pretty good. They gave me an easy way to find a hobby, save money and eat well and healthy. I hope you find some worth trying.

The recipes can be adjusted, fine-tuned, augmented and some ingredients can be substituted for based on your knowledge, outside advice, taste, etc. The recipes are derived from reflecting on meals I had at restaurants or friends homes or from magazines, TV shows and Internet queries. Some are from "scratch" as they say. Some have been galvanized through trial and error. If you like them thank God for the cooks whoever they may be. If you do not like them, thank God for the opportunity to know and to learn. Perhaps this book and its contents can help you kick-start a social gathering that is fun and rewarding. At least, it will help keep you from nightly "fast-Food" offerings and frozen dinners.

-Bill Kennedy

ABOUT MY RECIPES:

The recipes use a simple format. It is the same for all of them. The format is as follows:

1. Ingredients
2. Preparation
3. Presentation
4. Notes

Ingredients:

The ingredients used in making the dish can be adjusted. You can use less of an item or more. In some cases, you can substitute for an item. Perhaps, you do not like the recipe item or perhaps it is not available in a store or pantry. Usually, substitution should be limited to a seasoning type item or perhaps a vegetable with which you have a disagreement. Please, do not substitute Fish for "white Meat" or Pasta.

Preparations:

I follow what I have written in the recipe. Sometimes, I adjust or change the order. It is usually based on how my helpers are doing. The main dish is mine to prepare. I let my helpers have a glass of white wine while they help, provided they can avoid hurting themselves, others, or the meal.

Talk time with friends is priceless when you stop to think about it. A good time is had by all; a better time by all who help.

Presentation:

I make some suggestions as to what I try to do. You can use or change them. I think it is a good idea to ask someone special for a suggestion. In the final analysis, presentation is powerful. Have your camera ready to take pictures of the setting, the guests as well as the informal preparation activities.

Notes:

Finally, there is a "Notes" section at the bottom of each recipe. Make your changes in this area. You may want to change the cooking temperatures and times. All stoves, ovens and even the evil microwaves differ. You may want to adjust quantities or substitutions, etc. This can enhance using the recipe again. It may also lead to a new recipe for you as your "hobby" grows.

Final Final thought: *Don't Forget the Flowers or the Music*

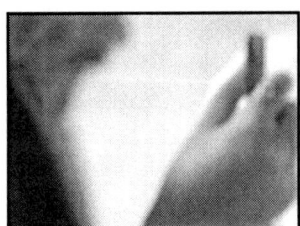  

Table of Contents

Hors d'oeuvres

Sauces, Soups & Salads

Sauces, Soups & Salads continued

Red Meat

White Meat

Fish

Pastas

Vegetables

Sandwiches

Breakfast

Desserts

Hors d'oeuvres

Salmon and Cream Cheese Triangles

Preparation

☐ Remove crust from bread slices

☐ In a bowl mix salmon spread with cream cheese

☐ Add capers, chives and 2 teaspoons lemon juice and mix

☐ In another bowl mix butter, salt, tarragon and 2 teaspoons lemon juice and lemon zest

☐ Spread salmon mixture on one slice of bread

☐ Spread butter mixture on a second slice of bread

☐ Place cucumber slices on buttered bread

☐ Place salmon slice of bread on top of cucumber-butter slice of bread

☐ Slice the sandwich diagonally to form 2 triangles

☐ Continue making sandwiches until salmon and butter mixtures are gone

Ingredients

1 loaf enriched white bread

4 ounces soft or whipped cream cheese

4 ounces whipped salmon cheese spread

2 teaspoons capers, minced

1 tablespoon chives, fine chopped

4 teaspoons lemon juice

Lemon zest (optional)

1/2 cup softened butter

pinch of salt

1 tablespoon chopped tarragon

1 cucumber, peeled and sliced into thin rounds

Presentation

Serve as an appetizer. Wine suggestions: Chablis, Riesling or Chardonnay.

Notes:

Stuffed Tomatoes

Preparation

The Filling:

☐ In a saucepan, thaw the spinach in boiling water, drain and set aside in a bowl

☐ Drain and rough chop artichoke hearts and add to spinach

☐ Add mayonnaise and butter, mix ingredients

☐ Add a pinch of salt and pepper

☐ Add Italian seasoning and Parmesan cheese, mix the ingredients

The Tomatoes:

☐ Cut the tops off the tomatoes and hollow out the inside of the tomatoes

☐ Fill each tomato with filling

☐ Add grated Parmesan cheese to the top of each tomato

☐ Sprinkle seasoned bread crumbs on top of the Parmesan cheese and then drizzle a little olive oil on top of the cheese

☐ To finish add a pinch of dry basil leaves to the top of each tomato

☐ Place the tomatoes in a 7" x 9" baking dish and add 1/4 inch of water to the baking dish

☐ Bake at 350 degrees for 5-7 minutes

Ingredients

Extra virgin olive oil

2 packages frozen spinach

15-ounce can artichoke hearts, rough chopped

4 tablespoons mayonnaise

2 tablespoons melted butter

1 teaspoon Italian seasoning

1 cup Parmesan cheese, grated

Salt and pepper to taste

Dry, crushed basil leaves

6 medium tomatoes

Presentation

Can be served as an appetizer or with a main course of fish or chicken.
Wine suggestion: Chablis or Sauvignon Blanc wine.

Notes:

Cantaloupe & Prosciutto with Honey-Basil Dressing

Preparation

☐ Slice prosciutto slices in half

☐ Make melon balls using a melon baller or cut into 2-inch slices

☐ Wrap melon with a slice of prosciutto, spear it with a toothpick to hold the ham

☐ Sprinkle with salt and pepper to taste

☐ Place dressed melon balls on a plate

Ingredients

1 cantaloupe or honeydew melon

1/4 pound prosciutto ham, sliced thin lengthwise

Kosher salt and crushed black pepper to taste

Toothpicks

Presentation

Drizzle honey-basil dressing around the plate and on the dressed melon balls. Serve additional dressing as a dipping sauce.

Honey-Basil Dressing Recipe:

In a blender, place 6-8 fresh basil leaves
Add pinch of kosher salt

Add 1/4 cup Champagne wine vinegar

Start the blender on low

Add 1/4 cup olive oil slowly

Add 2 tablespoons honey

Blend until smooth

Taste and adjust with salt and/or honey

Add a little olive oil to thicken if necessary

Notes:

Peach Bruschetta

Preparation

☐ Place peaches in pan of boiling water for 15 seconds

☐ Remove and skin the peaches, halve to remove pits and slice

☐ Spread melted butter on bread slices

☐ Sprinkle granulated sugar on bread

☐ Add peach slices in a single layer on top of bread slices

☐ Sprinkle more granulated sugar on peaches

☐ Place on baking sheet, cover loosely with foil

☐ Warm in 450-degree oven for approximately 20 minutes

☐ Remove, add powdered sugar and serve

Ingredients

2 whole peaches

2 teaspoons unsalted butter, melted

2 teaspoons granulated sugar

2 teaspoons powdered sugar

1 loaf multi-grain bread

Presentation

Serve as an appetizer.

Notes:

8-Layer Bean Dip with Tortilla Chips

Preparation

☐ On a cutting board smash garlic cloves and add a pinch of kosher salt; mash and mix together

☐ In food processor add garlic paste, both beans, chili powder, water, remaining salt and olive oil, blend until smooth

☐ Spread bean mixture evenly in a casserole dish

☐ Add a layer of shredded cheese on top of the bean mixture

☐ Mix and mash jalapeño peppers and avocados

☐ Spread the jalapeño/avocado mix over the cheese

☐ Add lettuce over the jalapeño/avocado mix

☐ Mix yogurt with chopped cilantro and add

☐ Mix tomatoes with the scallions and add

☐ Cover casserole dish, refrigerate until ready to serve

Presentation

Garnish with chopped cilantro. Drizzle fresh lime and lemon juices on top. Serve with tortilla chips. Wine suggestions: Cabernet or Merlot. Or serve with your favorite beer.

Ingredients

3 garlic cloves

2 teaspoons salt

15-ounce can black beans, drained and rinsed

15-ounce can pinto beans, drained and rinsed

2 teaspoons chili powder

2 tablespoons cold water

1 tablespoon extra virgin olive oil

2 cups shredded sharp Cheddar cheese

2 ripe avocados (Hass variety), peeled, halved and seeded

2 jalapeño peppers, sliced and fine diced

3 cups chopped romaine lettuce

2 cups plain, non-fat yogurt (Greek style if possible)

1/2 cup cilantro, chopped (reserve a small amount for garnish)

4 Roma tomatoes, rough chopped

5 scallions, thinly sliced

2 fresh limes

1 fresh lemon

Notes:

Black Bean & Mango Salsa

Preparation

☐ Combine all ingredients in a medium size bowl

☐ Cover with plastic wrap, let sit 30 minutes before serving

Note: refrigerate and serve chilled if desired

Presentation

Served as a dip, warm or chilled, with Tostitos chips or as bruschetta on diagonal slices of a French baguette. Salsa can also be served as a tropical salad on a bed of romaine lettuce either as a light lunch platter or as a side salad for a tuna or salmon dish.

Ingredients

- 2 mangoes, peeled and diced
- 1 can black beans, drained and rinsed or 1 cup cooked black beans
- 3 green scallions, finely chopped
- 4 Serrano peppers, seeded and finely diced
- 1/4 cup fresh-squeezed lime juice
- 2 tablespoons olive oil
- 3 tablespoons honey
- 1/4 cup chopped cilantro leaves, discard stems
- Kosher salt and crushed black pepper to taste

Notes:

Mango & Green Onion Salsa

Preparation

☐ Combine all ingredients in a medium size bowl

☐ Cover with plastic wrap, let sit 30 minutes before serving

Note: refrigerate and serve chilled if desired

Presentation

Served as a dip, warm or chilled, with Tostitos chips or as bruschetta on diagonal slices of a French baguette.

Ingredients

1 or 2 mangoes, peeled and diced

1/2 cup hydrated sun-dried tomatoes, diced

1/4 cup scallions, finely chopped

2 ounces fresh-squeezed lime juice

2 ounces olive oil

2 tablespoons fresh coriander, chopped

Salt and pepper to taste

Notes:

Bruschetta

Preparation

☐ Place tomatoes in a bowl and mix with olive oil

☐ Add garlic and basil, mix

☐ Cover mixture, refrigerate at least 1 hour

☐ Add shredded Parmesan cheese to mixture and serve

Presentation

Serve with warm slices of a French baguette or sourdough bread.

Ingredients

6 Roma tomatoes, sliced and seeded, then finely diced

2 tablespoons extra virgin olive oil

4 cloves garlic, minced

2 tablespoons dried basil

Shredded Parmesan cheese to taste

Notes:

Mango, Tomato & Red Onion Bruschetta

Preparation

☐ Combine all ingredients in a medium size bowl

☐ Cover with plastic wrap, refrigerate at least 30 minutes

☐ Serve chilled

Presentation

Serve as bruschetta on diagonal slices of a French baguette.

Ingredients

1 mango, peeled and diced

1 cup plum tomatoes, seeded and chopped

1/4 cup red onion, finely chopped

2 ounces fresh-squeezed lime juice

Salt to taste

Notes:

Salsa

Preparation

☐ Toss the tomatoes, scallions and red onions in olive oil and season with pepper

☐ Place the vegetables on a grill and char them, turning frequently

☐ Remove vegetables from grill and let cool

☐ Rough chop vegetables and mix them with remaining ingredients

☐ Refrigerate 2 hours, then serve

Presentation

Serve in a large bowl and sprinkle with green scallion pieces.

Ingredients

8 garden tomatoes, cut in half

1 red onion, cut into thick slices

1 bunch scallions (reserve a small portion of green part for garnish)

1/2 cup olive oil

1 teaspoon dry chipotle chili pepper (optional)

2 teaspoons cumin

2 teaspoons chili powder

1/2 cup cilantro leaves, chopped

2 teaspoons garlic, minced

4 limes, freshly squeezed

Notes:

Sauces, Soups & Salads

Honey-Basil Vinaigrette

Preparation

☐ In a blender, place 6-8 basil leaves (break or tear the leaves by hand)

☐ Add a pinch of kosher salt

☐ Add Champagne wine vinegar

☐ Start the blender on low

☐ Add olive oil slowly

☐ Add honey

☐ Blend until smooth

☐ Taste and adjust with salt, pepper and honey

☐ Add a little olive oil to thicken if necessary

Ingredients

6-8 fresh basil leaves

Kosher salt and crushed black pepper to taste

1/4 cup Champagne wine vinegar or a good-quality white wine vinegar

2 tablespoons honey

1/4 cup extra virgin olive oil

Presentation

Use as a salad dressing. Use over cantaloupe slices with Prosciutto as an appetizer.

Notes:

Tomato Sauce

Preparation

☐ Place tomatoes in blender and puree; add a little basil if desired, set aside

☐ In a large saucepan or pot, sauté onions and garlic in olive oil until soft

☐ Add salt, pepper, oregano, basil and stir

☐ Add tomato paste and water

☐ Bring to a simmer; simmer for 10 minutes over medium heat

☐ Add blended tomatoes and sugar and stir

☐ Bring to a slow boil over medium heat, then simmer over low heat for 2½-3 hours stirring occasionally

Note: if you wish to add meatballs, beef chunks, sausage, chicken pieces or pork chops, cook the meat first. Add the meat after the sauce simmers for 2 hours and continue cooking the sauce and meat together for 1 hour.

Ingredients

2 large cans Italian plum tomatoes with basil

2 small cans tomato paste

1½ cups water

2 large white onions, sliced or chopped

5 garlic cloves, minced

1 teaspoon oregano

1 teaspoon sweet basil

1½ tablespoons salt

1 teaspoon pepper

1 tablespoon granulated sugar

1/2 cup olive oil

Presentation

Use the sauce as a marinara sauce for rice dishes or pasta dishes. If meat was added to the sauce, use it as a meat sauce for spaghetti or other pasta dishes.

Notes:

Marinara Sauce

Preparation

☐ In a deep 10-inch fry pan, heat olive oil and gently sauté garlic

☐ Add tomatoes, tomato paste and sun-dried tomatoes

☐ Cook over medium heat for 20-30 minutes, stirring occasionally

☐ Add sugar

☐ Mix sauce with cooked pasta

☐ Make a chiffonade by rolling and then slicing basil leaves

☐ Add basil leaves to sauce and pasta

☐ Top with salt, pepper and grated cheese

Ingredients

4 tablespoons olive oil

5 garlic cloves, minced

2 - 28-ounce cans ready-cut and peeled plum tomatoes

6-ounce can tomato paste

4 tablespoons sun-dried tomatoes, chopped

1 tablespoon sugar

10 fresh basil leaves

Salt and pepper to taste

Grated Parmesan cheese

1 cup cooked pasta

Presentation

Serve with fish or chicken.

Notes:

Lemon-Butter Sauce

Preparation

□ Cook first three ingredients in a non-aluminum saucepan over medium-high heat for 5 minutes, whisking to mash lemons

□ Remove lemons

□ Stir in salt and next three ingredients, cook 10 minutes or until sauce has a syrup-like texture

□ Stir in whipping cream, cook for 1 minute

□ Reduce heat to low and gradually whisk in butter

□ Pour mixture through wire mesh strainer, discard pulp

□ Stir in parsley and serve immediately

Presentation

Serve with fish or chicken.

Ingredients

1 cup dry white wine

3 lemons, peeled and quartered

6 garlic cloves, minced

1 teaspoon kosher salt

1/2 teaspoon fresh-ground pepper

1/8 teaspoon Worcestershire sauce

1/8 teaspoon hot sauce

1/2 cup whipping cream

3/4 cup unsalted butter, sliced, room temperature

1 tablespoon fresh parsley, chopped

Notes:

Bordeaux Sauce

Preparation

☐ In a saucepan, over medium heat, combine wine and vinegar

☐ Bring to a boil

☐ Reduce heat to medium

☐ Cook until reduced to 1 cup, 30-35 minutes

☐ In another saucepan warm canola oil over medium heat

☐ Add shallot and sauté 3-4 minutes, stirring occasionally

☐ Add reduced-wine mixture

☐ Bring to a simmer and reduce heat to medium low

☐ Continue cooking, stirring until slightly thickened, 5-7 minutes

☐ Add thyme, salt and pepper, cook 2 minutes

☐ Add butter, whisk until smooth and blended

Ingredients

1 bottle good Bordeaux wine

2 tablespoons balsamic vinegar

2 teaspoons canola oil

1 shallot, finely minced

4 ounces chicken stock

1 teaspoon chopped fresh thyme

Salt and fresh-ground pepper to taste

4 tablespoons unsalted butter (1/2 stick), room temperature

Presentation

Serve with grilled New York strip steak or prime rib roast

Notes:

One-Hour Tomato Sauce

Preparation

☐ Sauté onion, pepper, basil and garlic in olive oil

☐ Add salt and pepper

☐ Place tomato paste and tomatoes in a second saucepan, stir

☐ Add water or stock and sautéed onion mixture

☐ Sauté 3 to 4 minutes, bring to a simmer

☐ Add sugar

☐ Simmer for 45 minutes, stirring occasionally

Presentation

Use as a topping for vegetable lasagna or pasta.

Ingredients

1 white onion, diced

1 green bell pepper, diced

8-10 fresh basil leaves, rolled and sliced thin like ribbon

6 garlic cloves, minced

1/4 cup olive oil

Salt and pepper to taste

1/2 cup tomato paste

4 garden tomatoes, seeded and diced

1 cup water or chicken stock

2 tablespoons sugar

Notes:

Pineapple Glaze

Preparation

☐ Cook all ingredients in a saucepan over medium heat whisking constantly, until consistency of syrup

☐ Yield: 1 cup

Ingredients

8-ounce can unsweetened crushed pineapple

1 teaspoon sugar

1 teaspoon cornstarch

Presentation

Serve over fish, steak or pork.

Notes:

Island Vinaigrette 1

Preparation

☐ Place all ingredients into a blender and puree

Presentation

Serve over fresh mixed greens. Optional: serve with diced chicken breast, garnish with mandarin orange slices and shredded fresh coconut.

Ingredients

1 mango or papaya, diced

2 garlic cloves, minced

1/4 cup fresh lime juice

3 tablespoons apple cider vinegar

3 tablespoons extra virgin olive oil

Notes:

Island Vinaigrette 2

Preparation

☐ Place first three ingredients into a blender and puree

☐ Mix chili powder with horseradish

☐ Add to fruit puree and blend

Presentation

Serve over fresh mixed greens. Serve as topping for oysters, shrimp, fried fish, cornmeal batter-dipped white fish or sea bass. Garnish with mandarin orange slices and shredded fresh coconut.

Ingredients

1 mango or papaya, diced

2 garlic cloves, minced

1/4 cup fresh lime juice

2 tablespoons red chili powder (ancho chilies)

1/2 cup fresh horseradish

Notes:

Ginger-Butter Sauce

Preparation

☐ In a sauce pan on the stove top combine soy sauce, honey, brown sugar, ginger, garlic and shallot

☐ Bring to a boil, then simmer for 5 minutes reducing ingredients by half

☐ Remove from heat and add butter cubes slowly while stirring

☐ Stir in Orange juice

☐ Place liquid in a blender and blend for 1 minute

☐ Remove and Strain into a serving bowl

☐ OPTIONAL: when finished, add a pinch of salt and a pinch of pepper and stir

Ingredients

1/4 Cup Soy Sauce (low sodium)

1/4 Cup Honey

1 Tablespoon light Brown Sugar

2 Teaspoons fresh Ginger, minced

2 Cloves Garlic, minced

1 Small Shallot, fine-diced

1 Orange, juiced

1/4 Stick of Butter, sliced in cubes

Presentation

Serve with your favorite seafood.

This is the perfect sauce to serve with Sea Bass with Honey-Soy Glaze found on page 80.

Notes:

Mango Carrot Sauce

Preparation

☐ Heat Canola Oil in saucepan or skillet.

☐ Add carrot, celery and onion.

☐ Saute until onion is translucent.

☐ Add Red wine.

☐ Add thyme and bay leaf.

☐ Add ginger, peppercorns and soy sauce.

☐ Add enough water to cover the vegetables.

☐ Cover and bring to a boil.

☐ Reduce heat and simmer for 1 hour.

☐ Strain mixture into saucepan.

☐ Add 1 pureed mango.

☐ Add butter, black pepper and salt.

☐ Cook over medium heat until mixture is reduced by 1/2.

Ingredients

1/4 cup canola oil

1 chopped or small-diced carrot

1 chopped or small-diced celery stalk

1 chopped, medium white onion

1 cup red wine

4 sprigs of thyme

1 bay leaf

4 thin slices of ginger

2 tablespoon black peppercorns

1 tablespoon soy sauce

1 medium mango

3 tablespoons unsalted butter

1 tablespoon black pepper

1 tablespoon salt

Notes:

Mango-Pepper Glaze

Preparation

☐ In a saucepan, combine red wine vinegar, sugar and peppercorns

☐ Cook over medium heat to reduce by half

☐ Strain sauce to remove peppercorns

☐ Puree mango in blender

☐ Mix mango puree and strained pepper sauce together

☐ Refrigerate until ready to use

Ingredients

1 large mango, peeled and diced

1 cup red wine vinegar

1/2 to 1 cup sugar

1/4 cup black peppercorns

1/2 cup extra virgin olive oil

Presentation

Serve either chilled or warmed in a pan on the stove. Serve as a topping for grilled or fried pork chops.

Notes:

Southwestern Tortilla Soup

Preparation

☐ In a large pot, combine the first seven ingredients

☐ Bring to a boil

☐ Add salt, pepper and cayenne pepper to taste

☐ Add crushed tortilla chips and cilantro leaves

☐ Bring to a boil again, then simmer for 10 minutes

☐ Strain vegetables and remove them

☐ Add zucchini, onion and chicken to the broth

☐ Boil until satisfied; season as you go

Presentation

Top with Monterey Jack and pepper cheese. Add tortilla chips, a few cilantro leaves and a slice or two of avocado.

Ingredients

4-6 cups chicken stock

1 small can tomato paste

1 cup carrots, diced

2 cups red onion, diced

1 cup celery, diced

1 cup corn kernels

2 cups red bell pepper, diced

Salt, pepper and cayenne pepper to taste

1 bag tortilla chips

1 bunch cilantro leaves

1-2 zucchini, sliced

1 onion, sliced

2-3 chicken breasts, cooked, diced

Monterey Jack cheese, julienned

Pepper cheese, julienned

Deep-fried tortilla chips, julienned from flour tortillas then fried

Avocado slices

Notes:

Stir-Fry Salad

Preparation

☐ Sauté the vegetables in hot olive oil

☐ Add garlic salt and pepper

☐ Watch the stir-fry; avoid over cooking

Presentation

Serve stir-fry al dente on a bed of mixed lettuce.

Add bacon bits as a topping.

Ingredients

1 cup baby carrots, julienned

1 each of red, green and yellow bell pepper, julienned

1 large red onion, julienned

1 cucumber, julienned

1 package mushrooms sliced

Garlic salt and crushed pepper

6 bacon slices, cooked crisp and crumbled

2 tablespoons extra virgin olive oil

Mix of lettuce: iceberg, Boston, etc.

Notes:

Antipasto Salad

Preparation

☐ Place cheese cubes and grapes on a platter

☐ Place meats, scallions and olives on another platter with crumbled Italian cheeses

☐ Place vegetables on a third platter

☐ Put various dips in ramekins

Presentation

Serve with various crackers and breads. Wine suggestions: Chardonnay or white zinfandel chilled;

Merlot or Chianti at room temperature.

Ingredients

Cheddar, pepper and Jack cheese cubes

Various kinds of olives, pitted and whole

Pepperoni and salami, sliced

Scallions

Red, yellow and green bell peppers, julienned

Various Italian peppers, whole

Celery sticks

Broccoli and cauliflower florets

Italian cheeses, crumbles or chunks

Red and white grapes

Blue cheese, sour cream, Dijon and honey mustard dips

Notes:

Warm Chicken Salad

Preparation

A. Prepare chicken:

□ Heat olive oil in fry pan over high heat

□ Add diced chicken, 1/2 teaspoon salt and 1/2 tablespoon pepper

□ Stir and turn chicken for 10 minutes or until light brown on all sides

B. Prepare salad dressing:

□ Use a glass bowl

□ Pour in balsamic vinegar

□ Add Dijon mustard

□ Add sugar

□ Mix and blend ingredients

C. Prepare salad:

□ Place arugula on serving plate

□ Sprinkle or crumble Feta cheese

□ Sprinkle grapes around the arugula

D. Assemble salad:

□ Pour dressing into fry pan with chicken

□ Add thyme

□ Add garlic

□ Add a little more salt and pepper (to taste)

□ Stir and toss 2-3 minutes

□ Ladle prepared chicken onto and in the middle of the arugula plate

□ Ladle extra sauce from pan over the salad

□ Serve

Note: add croutons if desired. To prepare croutons, dice Italian bread and brown in oven. Heat olive oil, balsamic vinegar and spices (your choice) in a pan; toss bread with heated mixture. Cool or let sit then serve.

Ingredients

- 1 pound chicken breasts, diced or cubed
- 1/2 teaspoon salt and 1/2 tablespoon pepper plus more to taste
- 1/4 cup olive oil
- 1/2 cup balsamic vinegar
- 2 tablespoons Dijon mustard
- 2 tablespoons sugar
- Arugula (Italian green leaves)
- Red grapes, sliced or halved
- Feta cheese
- 2 tablespoons fresh thyme
- 4 garlic cloves, chopped
- Croutons (optional)

Tuna Fish Salad

Preparation

☐ Drain tuna and place in large bowl

☐ Add 2 tablespoons mayonnaise and mix

☐ Add half of the onions and mix

☐ Sprinkle salt and pepper and mix

☐ Add pickles and half of the apples and mix

☐ Add pickle juice, 2 tablespoons mayonnaise and the rest of the onions and apples, then mix

☐ Add almond slices and mix

☐ Taste and add salt and pepper if needed

☐ Slice each garden tomato diagonally left to right and then cross left to right, avoid slicing all the way through cut it 3/4 through to open it like a flower

☐ Place tuna salad in center of open tomatoes

☐ Place tomatoes on lettuce leaves

Ingredients

2 cans chunk white or solid white tuna packed in water

Pinch kosher salt

Cracked pepper to taste

4 tablespoons mayonnaise

1 small yellow onion, diced

1 Red Delicious apple, peeled, sliced thin and diced

2 medium sweet pickles, sliced and diced

1 tablespoon pickle juice

2 tablespoons almond slices (optional)

Leafy lettuce

Garden tomatoes

Presentation

Serve with chilled Chardonnay. This salad also makes a nice sandwich on whole wheat or multigrain bread.

Notes:

Creamy Potato Salad with Dill Pickles and Capers

Preparation

☐ Place potatoes in a pot of cold water

☐ Heat and cook until fork tender, 20-30 minutes

☐ Drain water and reserve potatoes until they have cooled

☐ Boil eggs until hard, about 15 minutes. Cool, then peel, chop and reserve

☐ Slice scallion whites, reserve the green parts in a small bowl

☐ Add 2 tablespoons capers, half of the dill and a pinch of parsley to the green scallions in the bowl and reserve for use as a topping

☐ In a medium-large bowl mix mayonnaise, dijon mustard, red onion, sliced scallion whites, 2 tablespoons capers, the rest of the dill and parsley, dill pickles and pickle juice into a sauce-like state and reserve as mayo-mustard sauce.

In a large bowl add:

☐ Potatoes and eggs

☐ Coat the ingredients with the mayo-mustard sauce

☐ Add a little salt and pepper and stir

☐ Add the garnish (parsley, capers, green scallions and dill) and sprinkle on salad

☐ Add a little more pepper

☐ Squeeze the juice of a lemon over the salad

☐ Cover and refrigerate until ready to use

Ingredients

2½ pounds Yukon Gold potatoes, peeled and halved

2 eggs

Salt and pepper

1/4 cup Dijon mustard

5-6 scallions, chopped; reserve the green parts for garnish

4 tablespoons capers, drained

2 cups mayonnaise

1/2 cup dill pickles, sliced and chopped

2 tablespoons pickle juice

1/2 small red onion, finely diced

1/4 cup flat-leaf parsley, chopped; reserve a pinch for garnish

1/2 bunch fresh dill, chopped; reserve half for garnish

1/3 cup extra virgin olive oil for garnish

1 lemon

Presentation

Before serving, mix or toss first and then drizzle a little extra virgin olive oil on the salad. Wine suggestion: chilled white wine.

Notes:

Anise & Shallot Potato Salad

Preparation

☐ Bring 2 quarts of salted water to a boil

☐ Add potatoes to boiling water, boil until just tender, drain water

☐ Meanwhile, in a separate skillet, heat olive oil

☐ Add shallots and red pepper to hot oil

☐ Cook shallots and red pepper for 3 minutes, season with salt and pepper

☐ Transfer shallots and red pepper to mixing bowl

☐ Add potatoes

☐ Add vinegar and toss ingredients

☐ Cool salad to room temperature and add the fennel, anise or chervil

☐ Taste and add salt and pepper as needed

Ingredients

10-12 red (new) potatoes, sliced in 1/4-inch rounds

1/4 cup olive oil

1/2 cup minced shallots

2 tablespoons red pepper, diced

Salt and fresh black pepper to taste

2 tablespoons Champagne vinegar

1/2 cup anise, chervil or fennel leaves

Presentation

Serve warm or cold with entrée.

Notes:

Bill's Vegetable & Bean Soup

Preparation

☐ Use a Dutch oven with a tight lid

☐ Heat oil over medium-high heat

☐ Add onions, celery, carrots, bell peppers and garlic

☐ Sauté until the onions are soft or translucent, about 12 minutes

☐ Add both types of chili powder, coriander, cumin, oregano, basil and red pepper flakes, cook for 3 minutes

☐ Stir in tomatoes with their juice

☐ Add tomato paste and tomato juice

☐ Add 2 teaspoons each of salt and pepper

☐ Add stock, chick peas/garbanzo beans, cannelloni beans and lentils

☐ Add broccoli, zucchini and squash

☐ Bring pot to a simmer over high heat then decrease heat to medium high

☐ Simmer uncovered until the lentils are tender and the mixture thickens a little

☐ Stir often, cook 20 minutes more

☐ Taste and season soup with more salt and/or pepper if desired

Presentation

Serve in bowls, sprinkle some Parmesan cheese on top and add a little basil.

Ingredients

2 white onions, chopped

3 tablespoons extra virgin olive oil

3 celery stalks, cut in 1/2-inch slices

1 pound baby carrots or 3 large carrots cut in 1/2-inch pieces

1 red bell pepper, diced in 1/2-inch pieces

5-6 garlic cloves, diced

1/2 cup chili powder

1 tablespoon of Ancho chili powder

1 tablespoon ground coriander

1 tablespoon ground cumin

2 teaspoons dried oregano

1 teaspoon dried basil

1 tablespoon red pepper flakes, crushed

2, 15-ounce cans diced tomatoes with their juice

12-ounce can tomato juice

6-ounce can tomato paste

2 teaspoons kosher salt

2 teaspoons fresh-ground pepper

8 cups chicken or vegetable stock

2 16-ounce cans chick peas or garbanzo beans

2 16-ounce cans of cannelloni beans; drained and rinsed

1/2 cup dried green lentils

3 cups broccoli florets

2 zucchini, cut in 1/2-inch rounds

2 yellow squash, cut in 1/2-inch rounds

1/2 cup shredded Parmesan cheese

1/2 cup fresh basil leaves thinly sliced (chiffonade)

Bill's 6-Onion Soup with Parmesan Crostini

Preparation

☐ Use a large stock pot

☐ Melt butter over medium-high heat

☐ Add onions, leeks, shallots, scallions and garlic slices

☐ Cook until very soft, stirring occasionally

☐ Add chicken stock and heavy cream, cook 10 minutes

☐ Season with salt and pepper

☐ Puree the soup in a food processor or blender

☐ Use strainer or wire mesh sieve to remove and discard pulp

☐ The remaining liquid is the 6-Onion Soup

MEANWHILE:

☐ Preheat oven to 350 degrees

☐ Spread minced garlic on French bread slices

☐ Paint the slices with olive oil

☐ Bake until golden brown, about 5 minutes

Presentation

Float a French bread slice on top of each bowl of soup and sprinkle chive pieces around the edges of the bowls or in the soup. Grate a little nutmeg on top of the soup. Serve before the entrée.

Ingredients

4 tablespoons butter

2 yellow onions, diced or chopped

3 leeks, white part only; sliced lengthwise then crosswise

4 shallots, thin sliced

6-8 scallions, white part only, sliced in thin rounds

6 cloves garlic, sliced thin

1 teaspoon garlic, minced

4 cups low-sodium chicken stock

1 cup heavy cream

Kosher salt and white pepper to taste

1 tablespoon chives, chopped small

4 fresh French bread slices about 3 inches long

2 tablespoons grated Parmesan cheese

1/4 cup extra virgin olive oil

Nutmeg

Notes:

Tomato and Champagne Vinegar Salad with Basil Leaves and Feta Cheese

Preparation

☐ Place cherries in a large glass bowl

☐ Add cheese, onions and basil and mix

☐ Add vinegar and oil

☐ Sprinkle with salt and pepper to taste

☐ Add parsley and toss carefully

☐ Refrigerate until ready to use

Presentation

Place 4-5 leaves of romaine lettuce in a tall bowl. Place the mixed salad in the bowl and serve. Salad may also be served with a chicken breast, a tuna steak or a swordfish or salmon fillet.

Ingredients

6 cups cherry tomatoes, halved

3/4 pound feta cheese, cut into 1/4-inch cubes

1 small red onion, chopped

4 tablespoons Champagne vinegar or white wine vinegar

1/4 cup extra virgin olive oil

1 teaspoon kosher salt

1 teaspoon crushed black pepper

3 tablespoons fresh basil leaves, minced

3 tablespoons fresh parsley, minced

Notes:

Hot and Spicy Black-Eyed Pea Salad

Preparation

☐ Combine the peas with crumbled bacon

☐ Add 3 tablespoons bacon grease and mix

☐ Add the remaining ingredients in order listed above; mixing after each ingredient is added

☐ Cover and refrigerate overnight or at least several hours before serving

Presentation

Remove from refrigerator and toss carefully to combine all ingredients. In a large, tall bowl, place romaine lettuce leaves so that the bottom of each leaf meets in the center of the bowl. Place the tossed salad into the bowl and adjust the lettuce leaves so that they touch but are not overlapping. The ends should be upright.

Ingredients

5 cups or 2 cans of cooked, drained and dried black-eyed peas

6 bacon slices, cooked crispy and crumbled; save the bacon grease

1/2 cup extra virgin olive oil

1/2 cup red wine vinegar plus 3 teaspoons additional

1/2 cup red onion, chopped fine

1/2 cup red bell pepper, chopped fine

1/4 cup (more if you want) scallions, chopped fine

1/4 cup (less if you want) jalapeno peppers, chopped fine

2 teaspoons garlic, minced

2 teaspoons dry southwest seasoning (mix 1 teaspoon each: cumin, cayenne pepper, garlic powder, oregano, thyme, salt and pepper)

1 teaspoon kosher salt

2 teaspoons crushed black pepper

5 romaine lettuce leaves

Notes:

Chinese Chicken with Orzo-Pepper Salad

Preparation

☐ Use a small bowl to combine oil, vinegar, soy sauce and Hoisin sauce

☐ Whisk, cover with plastic wrap and reserve

☐ In a large bowl mix orzo, water chestnuts, chicken, onions and peppers

☐ Add sugar snap peas and toss

☐ Pour dressing over the mixture and mix to coat

☐ Garnish with toasted almonds and sesame seeds

☐ Cover with plastic wrap and refrigerate

Presentation

Serve chilled or at room temperature or serve warm.

Ingredients

9-ounce package frozen sugar snap peas, thawed

16-ounce package orzo, cooked, drained and reserved

1 cup water chestnuts, drained and chopped

3 cups chicken, cooked and diced

3 scallions, chopped

1 red bell pepper, chopped

1 green or yellow bell pepper, chopped

1/2 cup vegetable oil

3 tablespoons rice wine vinegar

2 tablespoons soy sauce

2 teaspoons Hoisin sauce

20-ounce package slivered almonds, toasted

Sesame seeds, toasted

Cucumber Salad

Preparation

☐ Peel and slice cucumbers in 1/4 inch rounds

☐ Add other ingredients except for dill and sour cream.

☐ Let the ingredients rest, covered and placed in refrigerator

Presentation

Before serving, mix the dill and dollup of sour cream in a dish then pour over the cucumber salad and mix.

Ingredients

2 cucumbers

1 teaspoon salt

1/2 white onion, chopped

1/2 cup white vinegar

2 teaspoons sugar

1/8 teaspoon sweet paprika

pinch of fresh dill

dollup of sour cream

Notes:

Red Meat

Green Apple Sauerkraut with Bratwurst

Preparation

☐ Remove sauerkraut from package, drain and dry it, set aside

☐ Heat 2 tablespoons of olive oil in large frying pan

☐ Add sweet onion slices and sauté for 3 minutes

☐ Add a third of the diced apples to the onions and sauté for 2 minutes

☐ Add ¼ cup white wine

☐ Add half of the sauerkraut

☐ Add 1 teaspoon caraway seeds

☐ Continue to sauté and toss or mix the sauerkraut and onions for 3 minutes

☐ Add remaining apples

☐ Add remaining sauerkraut

☐ Add 1 teaspoon caraway seeds

☐ Add ¼ cup white wine

☐ Add salt and pepper

☐ Continue to mix and toss for 3 minutes

☐ Remove from heat and pour into baking dish

☐ Add cumin, cayenne pepper and cinnamon

☐ Prepare brats separately boiling in water 5 minutes, then browning in frying pan 3 minutes

☐ Place cooked bratwursts on top of sauerkraut to bake

☐ Pour or sprinkle 1/4 cup white wine, pinch of salt, pinch of pepper and 2 teaspoons caraway seeds on top of bratwursts

☐ Cover dish with foil and bake at 375 for 20 minutes

☐ Remove foil and continue to bake at 375 until brown (about 10 minutes)

Ingredients

2 tablespoons olive oil

2 pounds sauerkraut (bag)

3 Granny Smith apples, peeled and diced

4 teaspoons caraway seeds

1 large sweet onion, sliced

Salt to taste

Pepper to taste

1 teaspoon cumin

1 teaspoon cayenne pepper

1 teaspoon cinnamon

6 bratwursts

3/4 cup white wine

Presentation

Serve with garlic or green onion mashed potatoes. Note: this dish can be prepared with various kinds of sausages, franks, pork chops or ribs.

Beef and Vegetable Stir-Fry

Preparation

☐ Snap ends off asparagus, cut spears into one-inch pieces, set aside

☐ Dredge stir in flour, set aside

☐ In a bowl, stir together soy sauce, water, garlic, 1 teaspoon sesame oil, hoisin sauce and crushed red pepper

☐ Heat remaining 2 teaspoons sesame oil in a large skillet over medium-high heat 2 minutes

☐ Add beef and carrots and stir-fry 4 minutes

☐ Add soy sauce mixture and stir-fry 1 minute

☐ Add asparagus, bell pepper, mushrooms and green onions and stir-fry 3 minutes

☐ Pour over hot rice and serve

Presentation

Serve with bread sticks and honey.

Wine suggestion: red zinfandel.

Note: if you omit the round steak and flour, this makes a nice vegetable stir-fry for a luncheon. Serve with a chilled white zinfandel or a buttery Chardonnay.

Ingredients

1 pound fresh asparagus

12 ounces top round steak, cut into strips

3 tablespoons all-purpose flour

1/4 cup light soy sauce

1/4 cup water

2 garlic cloves, minced

1 tablespoon dark sesame oil

1 tablespoon hoisin sauce

1/4 teaspoons dried, crushed red pepper

4 small carrots, cut diagonally into 1/4-inch slices

1 red bell pepper, cut into thin strips

1/2 cup fresh mushrooms, sliced

5 green onions, cut into 1-inch pieces

2 cups hot cooked rice

Notes:

South Western Treat
A Dry-Rub Marinade

Preparation

☐ Rub olive oil on both sides of meat

☐ Mix 1 tablespoon each of cumin, allspice and nutmeg together and rub on both sides of meat (you may want to double the amount of spices)

☐ Sprinkle red pepper flakes on both sides of meat

☐ Cover and refrigerate meat for 4 to 6 hours

Ingredients

Extra virgin olive oil

1½-2½ pounds flank steak

2 tablespoons red pepper flakes

1-2 tablespoons cumin

1-2 tablespoons allspice

1-2 tablespoons nutmeg

Presentation

Grill or broil flank steak for 5 to 6 minutes per side. Serve with new potatoes and garden salad. Wine suggestion: chilled red zinfandel.

Notes:

Flank Steak Roll-Ups

Preparation

In a bowl, mix 1/2 cup soy sauce, garlic, parsley, Parmesan cheese, pinch of salt and pinch of pepper, and southwest essence in sauce pan. Cook to reduce to half the amount of original volume

□ Pound or flatten flank steak to ¼-inch thickness and cut into one-inch wide slices

□ On a cookie sheet, coat the slices with reduced soy sauce mixture

□ Lay a bacon strip across the length of each steak strip

□ Roll up each steak strip with bacon on outside and place on a skewer

□ Brush roll-ups with soy sauce mixture and place on grill

□ Grill over medium heat, approximately 3 minutes per side

□ Make salad dressing by mixing together 1/4 cup soy sauce, shallots, diced garlic, pinch of salt, pinch of pepper and essence

Ingredients

3/4 cup soy sauce

6 garlic cloves, roasted

10 stems parsley, chopped

2 tablespoons grated Parmesan cheese

1 teaspoon salt

1 teaspoon pepper

Dash of southwest essence

1½ pounds flank steak

1/2 pound bacon

2 shallots, chopped

2 cloves garlic, diced

Mixed lettuce leaves and spoon spinach leaves

Cherry tomatoes

Olive oil

Presentation

Pour salad dressing on a bed of mixed greens and tomatoes, toss and serve with roll-ups.
Note: roll-ups can be used as an appetizer.

Notes:

Filet Mignon in Wine Sauce

Preparation

☐ Bring wine, chicken broth and beef broth to a boil

☐ Continue boiling, reduce until the solution is about half the original volume

☐ Heat 1 tablespoon olive oil in large fry pan over medium heat

☐ Salt and pepper steaks 1 teaspoon of each

☐ Sauté steaks until medium rare, about 4 minutes per side

☐ Transfer to platter and let rest for 5 minutes

☐ Add shallots, garlic, thyme, pinch of salt and pinch of pepper to skillet juices

☐ Stir 30 seconds and add 1½ cups of the reduced wine mixture to skillet

☐ Add butter and flour mixture and whisk until smooth

☐ Bring the mixture to a boil while stirring and scraping up scraps

☐ Boil until it thickens (coats a spoon), about 2 to 3 minutes

☐ Remove and pour over steaks

Ingredients

1 bottle red wine (merlot or Cabernet Sauvignon)

1 pint chicken broth or stock

1 pint beef broth or stock

2 tablespoons unsalted butter, softened

1 tablespoon all-purpose flour

1 tablespoon olive oil

6 6-ounce filets, 1½-inch thick

1 teaspoon salt

1 teaspoon fresh cracked peppercorns

1/4 cup shallots, chopped

1 tablespoon garlic, chopped

2 teaspoons fresh thyme

1 small bunch green onions

Presentation

Sprinkle parsley and chopped scallions on each plate.

Serve with spinach salad

Serve with herbed new potatoes and sherry dressing.

Wine suggestion: Merlot or Cabernet Sauvignon.

Notes:

Flank Steak with Pepper Sauce

Preparation

☐ Place 2 pounds flank steak in pepper marinade for 4 to 24 hours

☐ Place pepper sauce ingredients in blender and puree

☐ Warm sauce on low heat until ready to serve

☐ Grill steak 3 minutes per side on high heat

☐ Drizzle sauce on plate and over steak

Presentation

Serve with baked potatoes and vegetable medley.

Ingredients

2 pounds Flank Steak

Pepper Marinade:

2 tablespoons soy sauce

1 tablespoon Szechwan sauce

1 tablespoon peppercorns, crushed

2 tablespoons honey

2 tablespoons rice vinegar

Pepper Sauce:

1 roasted red bell pepper, peeled, seeded and roasted

1 green chili pepper, peeled, seeded and roasted

6 jalapeños, whole

2 Ancho peppers, dried

2 garlic cloves, minced

1 tablespoon fresh parsley, chopped

1 tablespoon fresh basil

1 tablespoon fresh cumin

2 tablespoons balsamic vinegar

1/4 cup olive oil

Notes:

Steak Au Poivre

Preparation

☐ Crack or crush peppercorns

☐ Brush Dijon mustard on all sides of the steaks

☐ Dip steaks in peppercorns

☐ Heat oil in fry pan until hot

☐ Cook steaks 4 to 5 minutes per side

☐ Add shallots, garlic, stock, cream and mustard in the order listed; add slowly while cooking steaks on first side

☐ After cooking, remove from heat, add 1/4 cup Grand Mariner and ignite

Presentation

After flambé process, serve with sour cream mashed potatoes, flavored baby carrots and long French beans.

Ingredients

4 New York strip steaks, 1½ inch thick

Mixed peppercorns, crushed

2 ounces Grand Mariner liqueur

1/4 cup Dijon mustard

2 tablespoons vegetable oil

1 shallot, diced

2 cloves garlic, diced

1 teaspoon salt

1 teaspoon pepper

1 cup chicken stock

1/4 cup cream

Notes:

Flank Steak Marinade

Preparation:

☐ Mix first seven ingredients together

☐ Place steak in large dish and pour in marinade

☐ Cover dish and refrigerate 2 to 24 hours

☐ Turn meat periodically, recover and refrigerate

Presentation:

Grill or broil flank steak for 5 to 6 minutes per side.

Ingredients:

1/2 cup soy sauce

3/4cup red wine (Cabernet Sauvignon)

Black pepper to taste

1 tablespoon fresh ginger, chopped

1/4 cup vegetable oil

3 cloves garlic, chopped

2 tablespoons brown sugar

2½ pounds flank steak

Beef Marinade

Preparation

☐ Mix ingredients together

☐ Place roast in large dish and pour in marinade

☐ Cover dish and refrigerate 2 to 24 hours

☐ Turn roast periodically, recover and refrigerate

Presentation

Use this marinade on any kind of roast. It can also be used as a meat sauce for spaghetti or other pasta dishes

Ingredients

1½ cups vegetable oil

3/4 cup soy sauce

1/4 cup Worcestershire sauce

1/2 cup red wine vinegar

1/2 cup fresh lemon juice

2 teaspoons salt

1 tablespoon pepper

1/2teaspoon chopped parsley

2 cloves garlic, minced

Italian Meatballs

Preparation

☐ Mix ingredients in bowl

☐ Form 1/2-inch balls

☐ Fry until brown in olive oil

Presentation

Serve with spaghetti or macaroni.

Ingredients

2 pounds ground chuck, lean

1½ cups Italian breadcrumbs

1/2 cup chopped parsley

3 cloves garlic, minced

2 eggs

¼ cup water

1 cup grated Parmesan cheese

Notes:

Bill's Red Wine Beef Stew with Bowtie Pasta

Preparations

Use a dutch oven with a tight lid

☐ Heat vegetable oil on medium-high heat

☐ Salt and pepper the meat

☐ Sear half of the meat pieces and set aside (cook for 8 minutes)

☐ Sear the rest of the meat pieces and set aside (cook for 8 minutes)

☐ Remove oil and wipe the inside of the pot, do not wash pot

☐ Melt butter in the pot

☐ Add onions and cook for 6 minutes

☐ Add garlic and cook for 1 minute

☐ Add tomato paste, stir and cook for 1 minute

☐ Add seared meat

☐ Add flour through a sifter to cover meat and onions, stir as it browns

☐ Add beef and chicken stock

☐ Add red wine

☐ Add bouquet garni

☐ Cover pot with lid

Transfer pot to oven

☐ Cook covered at 325 for 1½ hours

☐ Remove from oven

☐ Skim fat from pot

☐ Add potatoes, celery, carrots, peas, mushrooms and tomatoes

(continued on next page)

Ingredients

2½ pounds chuck roast from the shoulder, diced in 2-inch cubes

2 tablespoons unsalted butter

6 tablespoons vegetable oil

2 medium white onions, diced or rough chopped

1 pound baby carrots or 3 large carrots cut in 2-inch pieces

1 pound frozen large garden peas

3 stalks celery, cut in 2-inch pieces

12 button mushrooms, cut in halves

1½ pounds red potatoes, quartered

Bouquet garni - 2 bay leaves, 6 sprigs flat parsley and 6 sprigs fresh thyme tied with twine

Salt to taste

Crushed black peppercorns to taste

6 cloves garlic, minced or crushed

2, 15-ounce cans beef stock

2, 15-ounce cans chicken stock

1/2 bottle red wine

4 teaspoons sugar

1/4 cup all-purpose flour

3 tablespoons red wine vinegar

2 tablespoons tomato paste

23-ounce can whole tomatoes, cut or chopped and drained

Optional: 2 thin lemon peel slices, 4 orange peel slices

☐ Bring to a simmer on stove top and cook, uncovered, at medium-high heat for 1-1½ hours or until liquid thickens to taste or vegetables are tender

☐ Remove bouquet garni

☐ Stir in red wine vinegar, salt and pepper

Presentation

Serve over bowtie pasta or with garlic and chive mashed potatoes. Note: if using mashed potatoes, do not use red potatoes in the stew. Garnish options: grated Parmesan cheese; chopped flat-leaf parsley; chopped fresh chives; seasoned croutons; orange or lemon zest.

Notes:

Goulash and Bowtie Pasta

Preparation

☐ Using a heavy stew pot, fry bacon strips until fat is rendered, discard bacon

☐ Sauté onions in bacon fat, do not allow them to brown (add olive oil to keep from sticking if needed)

☐ Add beef, cover and cook 10 minutes until meat is browned, stir occasionally

☐ Add garlic and crushed caraway seeds (a pinch)

☐ Remove meat from heat

☐ Add paprika and stir

☐ Add enough warm water to just cover the meat

☐ Add bouillon cubes

☐ Cover pot and cook on low heat for 1 hour

☐ Add tomatoes after the meat has cooked for 1 hour

☐ Add green pepper

☐ Add a little more water and salt if needed

☐ Simmer for 30 minutes

☐ Add potatoes and cook for another 30 minutes

☐ Once goulash is done, dissolve sour cream and a little of the goulash sauce in a cup

☐ Add the mixture to the goulash

☐ Bring 4 quarts of water to a boil and add pasta

☐ Cook for 10minutes, drain, cover and set aside

Note: cook pasta when potatoes are added to the stew pot

Ingredients

2 slices bacon

2 Spanish onions, diced

1 tablespoon olive oil

2½ pounds chuck roast, cut for stew meat into 1-inch cubes

1-2 garlic cloves, chopped or crushed

Pinch caraway seeds, crushed

2 tablespoons sweet paprika

2 cups warm water

2 cubes beef bouillon

2 cans whole tomatoes, drained and chopped

1 green bell pepper, cut into strips

5 potatoes, peeled and cut into bite-size cubes

2 tablespoons sour cream

2 cups bowtie pasta

Presentation

Place the bowtie pasta on a plate and ladle the goulash on top. Serve Cucumber Salad (page 40) on the side. Serve with French bread.

Notes:

Mediterranean Meatloaf

Preparation

A. Make the dry mix
☐ In a food processor combine bread crumbs, black pepper, cayenne pepper, Ancho chili powder, chili powder, (optional: dry sage leaves and fennel seeds)

☐ Pulse until mixed

☐ Set aside in a bowl

B. Make the vegetable mix
☐ In a food processor combine onion, carrot, garlic cloves and red pepper

☐ Pulse until fine chopped but DO NOT PUREE

☐ Set aside in a bowl

C. Make the milk mix
☐ In a medium bowl whisk eggs, milk, mustard, hot sauce, marjoram, thyme, salt and pepper

☐ Set aside

D. Make the meatloaf
☐ Mix meats together

☐ Add vegetable mix

☐ Add dry mix

☐ Add milk mix. Note: if too moist, add more bread crumbs to the meatloaf

☐ Rub olive oil on sides and bottom of 9-inch loaf pan

☐ Place meatloaf in pan

☐ Cut out a one-inch slice of the loaf and reserve for later cooking letting the loaf expand while cooking

☐ Cover and place loaf pan in refrigerator for an hour

Ingredients

2½ pounds ground round, ground chuck, ground sirloin or a mixture of each

1 cup Italian bread crumbs

1 teaspoon ground black pepper

1/2 teaspoon cayenne pepper

1/2 teaspoon Ancho chili powder

1 teaspoon chili powder

Optional: 1 teaspoon dry sage leaves and 1 teaspoon fennel seeds; grind together with mortar and pestle

1/2 yellow onion, chopped

1 carrot, chopped

4 cloves garlic, whole

1/2 medium red pepper, diced

2 eggs

1/2 cup whole milk or half and half

2 teaspoons Dijon mustard

1 teaspoon hot sauce (Tabasco)

1 teaspoon marjoram

1 teaspoon dried thyme

Pinch of salt and pepper

1 cup ketchup

1/2 to 1 tablespoons ground cumin

3 dashes Worcestershire sauce

1 tablespoon honey

2 tablespoons brown sugar

1 tablespoon apple cider vinegar

2 tablespoons extra virgin olive oil

(continued on next page)

E. Make the glaze
☐ In a medium bowl combine ketchup, cumin, Worcestershire, Tabasco, honey, brown sugar and apple cider vinegar

☐ Mix to form sauce

☐ Cover and refrigerate

☐ Uncover loaf pan and place on cookie sheet

F. Bake the meatloaf
☐ Preheat oven to 350 degrees

☐ Cook for 1½ hours; after cooking for 15 minutes, baste the top of the loaf with some of the glaze

☐ After meatloaf is done, remove and let rest for 15 minutes before serving

☐ When ready, add more glaze to top of meatloaf and slice for serving

Presentation
Serve with mashed potatoes and French green beans. Garnish with olive slices and chopped flat-leaf parsley. Wine suggestion: Cabernet Sauvignon

Notes:

Beef Bourguignon

Preparation

☐ Brown meat in oil in skillet on stove, set aside meat

☐ Sauté carrots, mushrooms and onions for 5 minutes

☐ Put meat and vegetables in large pot

☐ Add flour to cover the meat and stir

☐ Add wine and water to cover the ingredients

☐ Add bay leaves, salt and pepper

☐ Cover pot and bring to a boil

☐ Reduce heat to simmer and cook until tender, about 2 hours

☐ Stir occasionally

Note: the liquid will evaporate until there is just enough for a sauce

Presentation

Consider serving bowtie pasta on a plate with Beef Bourguignon on top. Serve a side salad and French bread.

Ingredients

1/4 cup vegetable oil

2 pounds chuck roast (use upper-shoulder meat), cut into 2-inch cubes

2 carrots, peeled and sliced thin in round slices or diagonal

1 large white onion, diced

1 box (8 - 10) button mushrooms

1 tablespoon all-purpose flour

1 bottle red wine

1 bottle water (use the wine bottle)

4 bay leaves

Salt and pepper to taste

Notes:

White Meat

Spinach and Artichoke Raisin-Stuffed Pork Loin with Pine Nuts, Sweet Sausage and Mozzarella

Preparation

☐ In boiling water, cook frozen package of spinach for 18 minutes

☐ Drain spinach and dry

☐ Combine artichoke hearts and spinach in a large bowl

☐ Add Parmesan and ricotta cheeses and mix

☐ Remove casing from sausage; sauté sausage in oil in frying pan

☐ Drain fat, add sausage to spinach mixture and stir

☐ Add nuts, raisins, bread crumbs and balsamic vinaigrette and stir

☐ Butterfly pork loin and pound flat

☐ Add salt and pepper to both sides

☐ Stuff pork with filling

☐ Fold pork tightly and tie with butcher's string, leaving a 2-inch separation between ties

☐ Place pork on rack and place rack in roasting pan

☐ Pre-heat oven to 350 degrees

☐ Cook for one hour, baste pork with drippings several times during cooking

☐ Remove from oven

☐ Cut strings after pork has cooled, about 5 to 10 minutes after removing from oven

Ingredients

1 package frozen spinach

1 can (10 count) artichoke hearts, non-marinated, chopped

2 Italian sweet sausage links

1/2 cup shredded Parmesan cheese

8-ounce container ricotta cheese

2 tablespoons Italian bread crumbs

2 tablespoons raisins

2 tablespoons pine nuts

1/4 to 1/2 cup mozzarella, diced

1 tablespoon balsamic vinaigrette

1 pound center cut pork loin

Presentation

Make gravy using drippings in the roasting pan and 1/4 cup dry white wine in lieu of water; combine and add 1/4 cup flour, 1/8 teaspoon salt, 1/8 teaspoon pepper and 1/8 teaspoon red pepper flakes. Serve with wild rice or white rice with almond slivers. Serve with mixed greens and cherry tomatoes with a mustard, oil and balsamic vinaigrette dressing. Wine suggestion: chilled red zinfandel.

Chicken Milano with Herb Relish Garnish and Toasted Almond Green Vegetables

Preparation

Herb Relish:

☐ Mix tomatoes, onions, pimientos and basil in a medium bowl, reserve a little chopped basil or parsley for garnish

☐ Add the oil and both vinegars

☐ Add salt and pepper, mix

☐ Add cheese cubes, mix

☐ Cover and refrigerate

☐ Before serving stir to mix again

Chicken Cutlets:

☐ Heat large, nonstick skillet on medium-high heat and spray with a little olive oil

☐ Sauté chicken cutlets 3 to 4 minutes per side

☐ Add salt and pepper to cooked sides of chicken

☐ Cover with aluminum foil and set in warm oven

Toasted Green Vegetables:

☐ Heat nonstick skillet on medium-high heat

☐ Add almonds

☐ Sauté for 1 to 2 minutes, set aside

☐ Steam broccoli or asparagus in a steamer basket placed in a pot filled with 1 inch of water al dente

☐ Transfer to a bowl and add oil, salt and pepper

☐ Drizzle fresh lemon juice over vegetables

☐ Sprinkle almonds on top and toss

Presentation

Place warm chicken cutlets on a platter. Spoon herb relish over cutlets. Reserve some relish in a serving bowl for table use. Serve green vegetables.
Wine suggestion: red zinfandel or white Fumé Blanc.

Ingredients

Herb Relish:

1 cup diced plum tomatoes, drained and seeded

1/4 cup red onion, diced

1/4 cup drained sweet pimientos, sliced

1/4 cup packed, fresh basil leaves, rolled and cut (chiffenade)

1 tablespoon balsamic vinegar

1 tablespoon Champagne vinegar

1/2 pound feta cheese, fine cubed

Salt and pepper to taste

4 skinless, boneless chicken breasts, flattened or pounded to 1/2-inch thickness

3 tablespoons extra virgin olive oil

Toasted Almond Green Vegetables:

4 tablespoons sliced or slivered almonds

4 cups fresh broccoli florets or 1/2 bunch fresh asparagus tips or fresh haricot verts beans

3 teaspoons extra virgin olive oil

Salt and pepper to taste

Juice of 1 lemon

Baked Chicken and Rice

Preparation

☐ Mix soup, water, rice, paprika and pepper in a 2 quart casserole dish

☐ Place chicken on top of rice mixture, sprinkle with additional paprika and pepper

☐ Cover dish, place in oven

☐ Bake at 375 degrees for 45 minutes or until chicken and rice are done

Ingredients

1 can cream of mushroom soup

1 cup water

3/4 cup uncooked regular white rice

1/4 teaspoon paprika

1/4 teaspoon pepper

4 skinless, boneless chicken breasts

Presentation

Garnish with parsley and serve with warm French bread and chilled white wine

Notes:

Spicy Chicken with Black Bean Puree

Preparation

☐ Rub chicken with fajita seasoning

☐ Heat oil in skillet over medium-high heat

☐ Cook chicken for 3 minutes per side or until done

☐ Remove chicken from skillet and keep warm, reserve drippings

☐ Sauté onion and garlic in reserved drippings until tender

☐ Drain beans, reserve 2 tablespoons of liquid, rinse and drain beans again

☐ In a food processor, place onion mixture, beans, reserved liquid, tomatoes with green chiles, cayenne pepper, cumin, cilantro and lime juice, blend until smooth

☐ Remove mixture from food processor and put in saucepan

☐ Cook over medium heat, stirring constantly until thoroughly cooked

☐ Warm flour tortillas in skillet with a little olive oil

Ingredients

2-4 skinless, boneless chicken breasts

2 teaspoons fajita seasoning

1 teaspoon olive oil

1/2 cup white onion, chopped

2 garlic cloves, minced

15-ounce can black beans

10-ounce can diced tomatoes with green chiles

1/4 teaspoon cayenne pepper

1/2 teaspoon ground cumin

2 tablespoons fresh cilantro, chopped

1 tablespoon fresh lime juice

Shredded Monterey Jack cheese

Presentation

Place chicken on individual plates. Spoon a serving of bean puree next to each piece as well as a little on top of each piece. Place shredded Monterey Jack cheese on top of puree. Fold tortillas into quarters and place on plates.

Notes:

Grilled Herb Chicken

Preparation

☐ Pour olive oil and lemon juice in rectangular Pyrex or Corning Ware dish, stir

☐ Add salt and pepper, stir

☐ Add garlic, coriander, pepper flakes and oregano, stir

☐ 1/4 cup of the marinade is to be taken out of the dish for basting and set aside BEFORE marinating the chicken in the rest of marinade

☐ Place chicken breasts in marinade then turn them to coat the other side

☐ Cover dish with plastic wrap, set aside in refrigerator 1 hour before cooking

☐ When ready, place chicken breasts on a hot grill

☐ Grill for 2 minutes, turn chicken over and baste with marinade

☐ Grill for 2 more minutes, turn and baste

☐ Repeat process for a total cooking time of 10 minutes

Ingredients

4 skinless, boneless chicken breasts

1/4 cup olive oil

1/4 cup fresh lemon juice

Salt and pepper to taste

1 teaspoon garlic, minced

1/2 teaspoon ground coriander

1/8 teaspoon hot pepper flakes

2 teaspoons fresh oregano, chopped

1/4 cup hot melted margarine (optional)

Presentation

Place chicken on serving plate and baste with melted margarine. Serve with garlic mashed potatoes topped with chopped parsley. Other vegetable suggestions: green beans or stewed tomatoes. NOTE: this chicken is good diced and used with penne pasta or in a garden salad. It also makes a good chicken sandwich.

Notes:

Chicken and Apple Hash

Preparation

☐ Make mashed potatoes and keep warm

☐ Heat olive oil in frying pan and cook chicken, 4 minutes per side or until done

☐ Set aside, when cool, dice breasts

☐ Melt 2 tablespoons butter in frying pan, sauté peppers, onion and apples for 5 minutes, remove and keep warm

☐ Add 2 tablespoons butter, salt, pepper, diced chicken, parsley and thyme to frying pan and sauté for 5 minutes

☐ Remove from heat and make into chicken patties when cool enough to handle

☐ Heat 4 tablespoons olive oil or 4 tablespoons of butter in frying pan and cook patties for 1½ minutes per side)

Ingredients

2 - 4 boneless, skinless chicken breasts

1 large red onion, diced

3 Granny Smith apples, peeled and diced

2 - 4 red peppers, cleaned, seeded and diced

Salt and pepper to taste

8 tablespoons butter, or olive oil

6 sprigs fresh parsley, chopped

4 sprigs thyme

Nutmeg

Idaho potatoes

Presentation

Serve apple hash on top of chicken patties. Serve mashed potatoes. Dust nutmeg over potatoes and hash.

Notes:

Baked Chicken with Herbed Stuffing

Preparation

☐ Place 4-6 chicken breasts in skillet with olive oil and cook lightly on 375 heat for 4 minutes per side

☐ Place chicken in large baking dish (2 - 3 pieces on one end and 2 - 3 pieces on the other end)

☐ Mix stuffing with 1¼ cups boiling water and 4 tablespoons margarine

☐ Place stuffing in the middle of the dish so that chicken breasts are on either side of stuffing

Sprinkle paprika generously over the chicken

☐ Mix soup, milk and parsley together

☐ Pour soup mixture over chicken and stuffing.

☐ Bake at 400 degrees for 30 minutes

Ingredients

4 cups herb seasoned stuffing (like Pepperidge Farm brand)

4 - 6 skinless, boneless chicken breast halves

Paprika

1 can cream of mushroom soup

1/3 cup milk

1 tablespoon fresh parsley, chopped

Olive oil

Presentation

Serve with garlic mashed potatoes and long green beans seasoned with salt and pepper. Wine suggestion: chilled Chardonnay.

Notes:

Cajun Pork Chops

Preparation

☐ Mix crushed peppercorns with salt, cayenne pepper, paprika and garlic powder

☐ Rub pork chops in olive oil lightly and dredge in pepper/spice mixture

☐ Add herbed bread crumbs to both sides of chops

☐ Sauté chops in hot frying pan with olive oil, adding carrots, a little salt, thyme and 2 tablespoon of oil to chops as they fry for 5 minutes per side

☐ Transfer chops and carrots to a casserole dish and bake in oven at 350 degrees until done (about 1 hour)

☐ Keep chops warm at 200 degrees in oven

☐ Put carrots in a saucepan

☐ Add orange juice, cinnamon, nutmeg, parsley and brown sugar to pan and sauté for 5 minutes

☐ Pour carrot mixture over pork chops

STIR-FRY:
☐ Sauté onion in oil

☐ Add red and green bell peppers, snow peas, corn, salt and pepper

☐ Stir-fry until vegetables are crisp-tender

Presentation

Serve with wild rice and dried cranberries and blueberries. Serve stir-fry instead of salad

Ingredients

1 teaspoon each red, white, black and green peppercorns, crushed and mixed

1 teaspoon kosher salt

Salt and pepper to taste

1 teaspoon paprika

1 teaspoon cayenne pepper

1/2 teaspoon garlic powder

1 box herbed bread crumbs

4 - 6 carrots, pared and cut diagonally

6 sprigs fresh thyme, chopped

2 tablespoons cinnamon

1 tablespoon nutmeg

1 tablespoon dried parsley

2 tablespoons brown sugar

1/2 cup orange juice

1/4 cup extra virgin olive oil

4 thick pork chops on the bone

Stir Fry ingredients

1 white onion, chopped or sliced

1 each red and green bell peppers, julienned

1 frozen package snow peas

1/2 cup frozen corn

Ginger Pork Stir-Fry

Preparation

☐ Blend soy sauce, vinegar, oil, ginger and garlic in bowl

☐ Add pork to mixture

☐ Marinate 10 minutes

☐ Spray large skillet with cooking spray

☐ Heat skillet over medium-high heat

☐ Add pork, stir-fry 3 minutes

☐ Stir water and vegetables into mixture

☐ Cover and cook 5 minutes or until vegetables are crisp-tender

Ingredients

1 pound boneless pork loin, cut into 3/4-inch cubes

1 tablespoon soy sauce

1 tablespoon vinegar

1 teaspoon sesame oil

1/2 teaspoon ginger

1 garlic clove, minced

1 tablespoon water

16-ounce package frozen stir-fry vegetables, or make your own

Presentation

Garnish with sesame seeds.

Wine suggestion: chilled Chardonnay.

Notes:

Oven-Baked Pork Loin with Herb Dressing

Preparation

☐ In a bowl, mix the first seven ingredients

☐ Rub olive oil over pork

☐ Coat pork with mixed ingredients

☐ Place pork in baking rack and place rack in baking pan

☐ Place pork in oven and cook at 350 degrees until done, approximately 30 minutes or until thermometer reads 160 degrees at the thickest part of the meat

Presentation

Serve with sour cream mashed potatoes and long green beans. Wine suggestion: red zinfandel

Ingredients

1 cup fine bread crumbs

1 - 2 tablespoons Dijon mustard

1 tablespoon dried thyme

1 tablespoon dried rosemary

2 tablespoons fresh, shredded horseradish

2 garlic cloves, minced

Kosher salt and fresh ground peppercorns to taste

2 - 2½ pounds pork loin, remove excess fat

1/4 cup extra virgin olive oil

Notes:

Pork Tenderloin Roulade
with Black Bean Sauce

Preparation

MARINADE:

☐ Mix garlic, soy sauce, orange juice and pineapple juice

☐ Set aside in the refrigerator for 1 hour

STUFFING:

☐ Blend plantains, egg white, diced ham and scallions in a blender

☐ Add seasoned breadcrumbs, blend to thicken

MEAT PREPARATION:

☐ Place flattened pork in a large dish and season with salt and pepper

☐ Stuff with stuffing, then roll and tie pork with string

☐ Pour marinade over pork and refrigerate one hour

☐ Place pork on rack in pan and brush with melted butter

☐ Cook at 400 degrees until done, about 40 minutes (20 minutes per pound)

☐ Remove and let sit for 10 minutes, then carve and serve

Ingredients

1½ pound pork tenderloin, trim fat and butterfly lengthwise

Kosher salt and crushed black pepper to taste

3 garlic cloves, chopped fine

1/4 cup soy sauce

1/4 cup orange juice

1/4 cup pineapple juice

2 plantains, chopped

1 egg white

1/2 - 1 cup diced ham

1/4 cup scallions

1/2 cup seasoned breadcrumbs

4 tablespoons melted butter

Presentation

Serve with black bean sauce, julienned vegetables, rice and mango salsa.
Wine suggestion: chilled Chardonnay.

Notes:

Veal Piccata

Preparation

☐ Mix flour and Vege-Sal together, set aside

☐ On a cutting board, pound veal pieces evenly on both sides, cut into 2-inch pieces

☐ Dredge veal through flour mixture

☐ In a nonstick frying pan, add butter over medium heat

☐ Add veal pieces and cook 5 minutes, continuously shaking pan and turning meat to avoid burning the meat

☐ Remove pork and place on serving platter in 200 degree oven until needed

☐ Deglaze frying pan by adding white wine, lemon juice, water, tarragon and capers

☐ Stir over medium heat an additional 5 minutes or until sauce reduces and is the consistency of a medium white sauce

☐ Pour sauce over veal and serve

Ingredients

1/2 - 1 pound veal scallopini

2 tablespoons all-purpose flour

2 teaspoons Vege-Sal

2 tablespoons capers

1/4 cup butter

1/2 cup white wine

1/4 cup fresh squeezed lemon juice

1/2 cup water

2 tablespoons dried tarragon

Presentation

Garnish with chopped fresh parsley, watercress and thin slices of lemon. Serve with sour cream or almond mashed potatoes and a garden salad topped with cherry tomato halves and oil and red wine vinaigrette dressing.

Notes:

Veal Marsala

Preparation

Prepare mushrooms:

☐ Heat olive oil in frying pan over medium heat

☐ Add 1 tablespoon butter and mushrooms

☐ Add Marsala wine and cook for 2 minutes, set aside and reserve until needed for deglazing

Prepare veal:

☐ Mix flour and Vege-Sal together, set aside

☐ On a cutting board, pound veal pieces evenly on both sides, cut into 3 or 4 inch pieces

☐ Dredge veal through flour mixture

☐ In a nonstick frying pan, add butter over medium heat

☐ Add veal pieces and cook about 5 minutes, continuously shaking pan and turning meat to avoid burning the meat

☐ Remove meat and place on serving platter in 200 degree oven until needed

☐ Deglaze frying pan by adding chicken stock, wine, and a little more butter

☐ Mix in separate bowl flour mixture of 1/4 cup cold water, 1/4 cup flour then add to frying pan

☐ Stir to reduce

☐ While reducing, add mushrooms and cook for 2 minutes

☐ Pour sauce over veal and serve

Ingredients

- 1/2 - 1 pound veal scallopini
- 2 tablespoons all-purpose flour
- 2 teaspoons Vege-Sal (optional)
- 1 cup sliced mushroom caps
- 1/4 cup butter
- 1/2 cup chicken stock
- 1/2 cup Marsala wine

Presentation

Garnish with chopped fresh parsley. Serve with sour cream or hazelnut mashed potatoes, asparagus spears and a garden salad topped with cherry tomato halves and oil and red wine vinaigrette dressing.

Notes:

Caribbean Pork Chops

Preparation

The day before serving:

☐ Mix paprika, cumin, and allspice together, rub on both sides of pork chops

☐ Place chops in baking dish and cover each chop with brown sugar

☐ Cover baking dish with plastic wrap and refrigerate 24 hours

☐ The day you serve:

☐ Slice tomatoes in half, remove seeds

☐ Slice peppers into quarters or strips, removing seeds as you slice

☐ Peel and slice red onions

☐ Cut pineapple into wedges of various lengths

On the grill:

☐ Sear pork chops on high heat, then grill on low heat; watch carefully and turn frequently

☐ After 10 minutes, place chops toward back of grill to keep warm

☐ Add peppers and onions to grill, turning several times

☐ When peppers begin to show grill marks, add pineapple wedges and tomatoes

☐ Grill fruit and vegetables to your satisfaction

Ingredients

2 teaspoons paprika

2 teaspoons cumin

2 teaspoons allspice

2 cups brown sugar

2 green peppers

2 red peppers

2 yellow peppers

8 Roma tomatoes

2 Bermuda onions (red)

Rice or couscous (optional)

4-6 thick pork chops on the bone (1 - 2 inches thick)

1 whole pineapple

Presentation

Serve with rice or couscous. Wine suggestions: serve with Merlot or Chardonnay.

Notes:

Grilled Pork Chops with Rosemary

Preparation

☐ Combine first seven ingredients in a bowl or a plastic bag

☐ Add pork chops and coat with marinade

☐ Place in refrigerator for 8 to 24 hours, turning chops occasionally

☐ Before grilling, let chops stand at room temperature 30 minutes

☐ Remove chops from marinade, discard marinade

☐ Grill chops, with grill cover down at 350 to 400 for 12 minutes, turning occasionally until done

Ingredients

1/4 cup extra virgin olive oil

1/4 cup balsamic vinegar

1 tablespoon dried rosemary

1 tablespoon fresh lime juice

1/4 teaspoon freshly ground pepper

2 garlic cloves, minced

1 green onion, chopped

4 - 6 thick-cut pork chops on the bone

1 bunch scallions, sliced 1/8 inch thick

Presentation

Garnish with scallions. Serve with new potatoes and almond-flavored long green beans. Wine suggestion: red zinfandel.

Notes:

Fish

Salmon Fillo With Red Wine Sauce

Preparation

Salmon Steaks:

☐ Lay out 2 sheets of fillo, one on top of the other

☐ Brush inside of dough with 8 tablespoons melted butter

☐ Place salmon steak on buttered side of dough

☐ Wrap dough around salmon

☐ Cut off the ends of the dough to expose the ends of the salmon and brush with butter

☐ Repeat for additional salmon steaks

☐ Heat olive oil in fry pan over medium high heat

☐ Add salmon wraps and cook 30 seconds per side

☐ Remove and place wraps on baking sheet

☐ Pre-heat oven to 450 degrees

☐ Bake salmon for 5 minutes, or until done

Red Wine Sauce:

☐ Put red wine in sauce pan and warm over medium high heat to reduce by 1/3

☐ Add wine vinegar and shallots

☐ Reduce mixture, stirring frequently

☐ Add 4 tablespoons butter while reducing, whisk constantly until done

☐ Pour sauce in center of plates and place salmon in middle of sauce

Ingredients

4, 6-ounce salmon steaks

Fillo dough, 2 sheets per steak

1 cup red wine

1/4 cup red wine vinegar

2 medium shallots, finely chopped

12 tablespoons unsalted butter

Extra virgin olive oil

Salt and pepper

Green onions, chopped (for garnish)

Parsley (for garnish)

Presentation

Garnish with chopped green onions and/or parsley. Serve with rice and asparagus.

Notes:

Grilled Salmon with Honey Mustard Dill Sauce

Preparation

☐ Sprinkle a total of 1/4 teaspoon salt and 1/4 teaspoon pepper on both sides of steaks

☐ Combine remaining salt and pepper, yogurt, and next 4 ingredients in a small bowl, stir well and set aside

☐ Spray grill with cooking spray, turn on high heat

☐ Grill steaks for 6 minutes per side or until fork tender

☐ Top with honey mustard dill sauce and serve

Presentation

Serve with sour cream mashed potatoes, cherry tomato halves, and fresh asparagus spears.
Wine suggestion: chilled Chardonnay.

Ingredients

1/2 teaspoon salt

1/2 teaspoon pepper

4, 6-ounce salmon steaks about 1-inch thick

1 cup plain low-fat yogurt

1/4 cup fresh dill, chopped

2 tablespoons green onions, minced

1½ tablespoons Dijon mustard

2 teaspoons honey

Cooking spray

Notes:

Grilled Tuna With Mango Carrot Sauce

Preparation

☐ Combine first 8 ingredients in a bowl, stir well and set aside

☐ Sprinkle a total of 1/4 teaspoon salt and 1/4 teaspoon pepper over steaks

☐ Spray grill with cooking spray, turn on high heat

☐ Grill steaks 4 minutes per side or until done to taste on high heat

☐ Top with mango carrot sauce (page 26)

Presentation

Serve with sour cream mashed potatoes, cherry tomato halves and fresh broccoli with wine sauce. Garnish plate with fresh pineapple wedges.
Wine suggestion: chilled Sauvignon Blanc.

Ingredients

1/4 cup mango, peeled and diced

1 cup carrots, julienned

3 tablespoons fresh lime juice

1 tablespoon fresh chives, minced

1/4 teaspoon crushed red pepper

1/8 teaspoon kosher salt

1/8 teaspoon coriander

1/8 teaspoon cumin

1/4 teaspoon salt

1/4 teaspoon black pepper

4, 6-ounce yellowfin tuna steaks about 1-inch thick

Notes:

Tuna Steak

Preparation

□ Rub tuna with oil or brush with Dijon mustard

□ Dredge steak in peppercorns, covering all sides and edges

□ Heat sesame oil over medium heat in skillet

□ Sear tuna in hot skillet

□ Add wine and cook tuna 3 minutes per side

□ Remove from heat, slice into pieces 1/2-inch thick by 2-inches long

□ Put tomatoes and avocado in a bowl

□ Add salt, pepper, lemon juice, 2 tablespoons sesame oil and cilantro, mix

Presentation

Per serving: place one lettuce leaf on a plate. Place 3 tablespoons of tomato/avocado mix on top of the lettuce. Place 3 tuna slices on top of tomato/avocado mix. Garnish with chives.

Ingredients

1 tuna steak, 6 inches x 2 inches x 2 inches

1/2 cup crushed black peppercorns

2 tablespoons sesame oil

Dijon mustard

1 package cherry tomatoes diced

1 avocado, diced

Juice of 1 lemon

6 cilantro leaves, chopped

Salt and pepper to taste

Large romaine lettuce leaves

fresh chives chopped for garnish

1/4 cup white wine

Notes:

Grilled Swordfish With Balsamic Onion Sauce

Preparation

☐ In a large non-stick skillet coated with cooking spray, or heat olive oil over medium heat

☐ Add onion, garlic and bay leaf, sauté 8 minutes or until tender

☐ Add water and next 4 ingredients; cover and simmer 2 minutes

☐ Remove bay leaf from balsamic onion sauce

☐ Sprinkle salt and pepper over fillets

☐ Spray grill with cooking spray and turn grill on high

☐ Grill 4 minutes per side or until done

☐ Top fillets with balsamic onion sauce and serve

Presentation

Serve with sour cream mashed potatoes, cherry tomato halves and fresh asparagus spears.
Wine suggestion: chilled Chardonnay.

Ingredients

1 teaspoon extra virgin olive oil

2 cups onion, chopped

1 clove garlic, minced

1 bay leaf

1/4 cup water

3 tablespoons balsamic vinegar

1½ tablespoons tomato paste

1/8 teaspoon kosher salt

1/8 teaspoon pepper

4, 6-ounce swordfish steaks about 1-inch thick

1/2 teaspoon pepper

1/4 teaspoon kosher salt

Notes:

Grilled Salmon Steaks With Tarragon Sauce

Preparation

Salmon:

☐ Spread 2 tablespoons mayonnaise and 2 tablespoons tarragon on steaks

☐ Grill steaks at 350-400 degrees with grill lid down 10 minutes or until salmon flakes easily with fork

☐ Sprinkle with lemon juice

☐ Serve with tarragon sauce and lemon wedges

Tarragon Sauce:

☐ Combine yogurt, Dijon mustard, 2 tablespoons mayonnaise and 1½ teaspoons tarragon

☐ Chill until ready to serve

Ingredients

4, 8-ounce salmon steaks

4 tablespoons mayonnaise

2 tablespoons plus 1½ teaspoons dried tarragon

1 tablespoon fresh lemon juice

Lemon wedges

2 tablespoons plain low-fat yogurt

1/2 teaspoon Dijon mustard

Presentation

Serve salmon steaks with sauce on top and lemon wedges for garnish.
Wine suggestion: chilled Chardonnay.

Notes:

Sea Bass with Honey-Soy Glaze and Ginger-Butter Sauce

Preparation

☐ Preheat oven to 350 degrees

☐ Combine vinegar, soy sauce and honey in small saucepan over high heat

☐ Mix 1 tablespoon cold water and cornstarch in small bowl whisk into soy mixture

☐ Bring to a boil, stirring constantly

☐ Reduce heat to medium and simmer, stirring constantly, about 2 minutes until mixture thickens to a glaze

☐ Pour 1/2 cup glaze into shallow baking dish

☐ Add fish; turn to coat all sides with glaze

☐ Place coated fish on a baking sheet or tray

☐ Bake 18 minutes or until done

☐ While fish is baking, prepare Ginger-Butter Sauce (on page 25)

☐ After baking spoon remaining glaze over fish and place under broiler

☐ Broil until glaze is bubbling and begins to caramelize, about 2 minutes

☐ Using a spatula, place fish on plates

☐ Serve with ginger butter sauce

Ingredients

4, 6-ounce sea bass fillets
Honey-Soy Glaze
1/2 cup rice vinegar
1/4 cup soy sauce
1/4 cup honey
1 tablespoon cold water
2½ teaspoons cornstarch
Ginger-Butter Sauce
Recipe on page 25

Presentation

Spoon or ladle a pool of the Ginger-Butter Sauce into the center of each plate.
Place the prepared fillets on the ladled sauce. Drizzle a little sauce over the fillets and around the rim of each plate

OPTIONAL GARNISH: Sprinkle toasted black and white sesame seeds over the fillets and around the rim of the plate. Place 3 chive stems in any arrangement over each fillet

Serve with new potatoes and almond-flavored long green beans.

Wine suggestion: Red Zinfandel.

Notes:

Peppered Swordfish Steaks

Preparation

Mashed Potatoes:

☐ Make mashed potatoes

☐ Add chopped scallions to potatoes and stir

☐ Place bowl in warm oven until ready to serve

☐ Swordfish Steaks:

☐ Rub olive oil on both sides of fish

☐ Brush Dijon mustard on all sides and edges of fish

☐ Dip coated steaks in crushed peppercorns to coat entire steak

☐ Heat 1/4 cup oil in fry pan over medium high heat

☐ Cook steaks 3 to 4 minutes per side

☐ Optional: add wine to pan while steaks cook

Vegetables:

☐ Add vegetables, salt and pepper to pot of boiling water

☐ Blanch 3 to 5 minutes

☐ Remove vegetables and place in sauce pan with 2 tablespoons olive oil, pinch of salt and 1 tablespoon pepper

☐ Cover and cook over medium heat 5 to 10 minutes or until done to taste

Ingredients

2 to 4 swordfish steaks, 1 to 1½-inches thick

1/4 cup white wine (optional)

Dijon mustard

1 cup crushed black peppercorns

Olive oil

4 Idaho potatoes, peeled and chopped for making mashed potatoes

1 bunch scallions, chopped

2 cups baby carrots

1 zucchini, sliced in 1/8-inch rounds

1 squash, sliced in 1/8-inch rounds

Half stick melted butter

1/2 bunch parsley, chopped

1 bunch scallions, green and white parts, chopped

Presentation

Serve steaks while hot. Put vegetables and potatoes on each plate. Drizzle melted butter and sprinkle parsley on top of vegetables. Garnish potatoes with green scallions. Garnish steaks with white scallions. Wine suggestion: chilled Sauvignon Blanc.

Notes:

Salmon With Limes

Preparation

Pineapple with marinade:

☐ Mix light and dark rum, cinnamon, Allspice, brown sugar, butter and honey in a pot and heat over medium heat until warm

☐ Place pineapple pieces on wooden skewers, dip skewers in marinade

☐ Grill pineapple 2 to 3 minutes over medium heat, watch and turn from side to side

☐ Remove from grill

☐ Place on serving plate and pour remaining marinade over pineapple

Shrimp Appetizer:

☐ Puree mango or papaya with olive oil, lime juice and orange juice

☐ Soak shrimp in the mango puree for 15 minutes (minimum)

☐ Grill shrimp and lime slices 5 minutes over high heat

Salmon Dressing:

☐ Puree onion, olive oil, balsamic vinegar, Tabasco, honey and lime juice in a blender

☐ Put puree and wine in a sauce pan and heat over medium heat for 20 minutes to reduce puree to syrup consistency

Note: reserve a portion of the dressing to pour over salmon after grilling, use remaining dressing for basting salmon while grilling

(Continued on next page)

Ingredients

4 Salmon steaks (optional: Mahi Mahi or Red Snapper)

Salt and pepper to taste

1/4 cup olive oil

4 limes, sliced

1 red and 1 green pepper sliced

Pineapple with marinade:

1 fresh pineapple, remove outer husk and inner core, slice pineapple into 2-inch squares

8 tablespoons butter, melted

1/2 cup brown sugar

3 tablespoons honey

1/4 cup each light and dark rum

1 tablespoon cinnamon

1/2 tablespoon Allspice

Shrimp Appetizer:

Shrimp, cleaned and deveined, approximately 5 per serving

2 limes, sliced

1 mango or papaya

1/4 cup olive oil

Juice from 1 lime

1 cup orange juice

Salmon Dressing:

1/4 cup olive oil

1/4 cup balsamic vinegar

2 tablespoons Tabasco

1 tablespoon honey

2 medium sweet onions, sliced, grilled

1/2 cup white wine

Juice from 1 lime

Main Course Preparation:

☐ Drizzle olive oil over fish, add salt and pepper

☐ Grill over high heat 1 minute per side

☐ Baste or pour salmon dressing on one side, cook 2 to 3 minutes, turn fish and repeat*

☐ Grill lime slices and red and green pepper slices

*Note: cooking time is approximately 4 minutes per inch thickness of fish—watch to avoid drying out fish

Presentation

1. Serve shrimp and limes as an appetizer

2. Serve pineapple slices as a fruit salad with the main course

3. Serve salmon with lime slices and grilled peppers. Pour reserved salmon dressing on top of salmon.

Notes:

Tuna Tubeki

Preparation

☐ Prepare pasta in 4 quarts of water with salt and olive oil

☐ Place cooked pasta in large bowl

☐ Mix in tuna and peas

☐ Add lemon juice, mix

☐ Add green olive paste, cherry tomatoes, and pepper, mix

☐ Garnish with parsley

Presentation

Serve with chicken or fish and Radar's Rice (page 100). Note: add 2 tablespoons Worcestershire and 1 teaspoon cayenne pepper if you want to make Radar's Hot Rice

Ingredients

1-pound bag pasta tubes

10-ounce bag frozen peas, cooked

1 jar green olive paste with garlic or pesto paste

Juice of 2 lemons

2 cans solid white tuna packed in water, drained

1 package cherry tomatoes

1/4 cup olive oil

2 teaspoons crushed black pepper

1 teaspoon salt

Italian parsley chopped for garnish

Notes:

Red Sauce – White Fish

Preparation

☐ Combine red sauce ingredients in blender

☐ Place mixture in sauce pan

☐ Cook over high heat to reduce slightly

☐ Bake fish with salt, pepper and a little lemon juice for approximately 20 minutes until flakes when forked

Presentation

Serve sauce warm over a baked white fish.

Ingredients

4 - 6 white fish filets

Red Sauce ingredients

1 - 2 peeled and grilled red peppers

4 cloves garlic, minced

Salt and pepper to taste

1/4 - 1/2 cup olive oil

2 tablespoons horseradish, freshly grated

4 dashes Tabasco

1 teaspoon dried tarragon

Notes:

Pastas

Green Chili Macaroni

Preparation

☐ Cook the macaroni about 10 minutes and set aside

☐ Oven-roast 3 or 4 poblano peppers about 10 minutes then peel, seed and use food processor to puree (add a little water or oil while making the puree)

☐ Dice red pepper, red onion and poblano pepper

☐ Grate the hot pepper Jack cheese

☐ Heat oil in a heavy pan over high heat and sauté the garlic and diced peppers and onion until tender

☐ Add corn kernels and sauté quickly

☐ Add the cooked macaroni, poblano puree, cream and cheese

☐ Stir until all the ingredients are thoroughly mixed

☐ Season to taste and serve

Presentation

Serve warm or cold with entree.

Serve cold as an appetizer.

Ingredients

1 tablespoon of corn, canola or other vegetable oil

1/4 cup diced poblano peppers

1/2 cup diced red bell peppers

1/2 cup diced red onion

1 tablespoon garlic, minced

1/2 cup sweet corn kernels

2 cups cooked elbow macaroni (al dente)

1/2 cup roasted, peeled and pureed poblano peppers (3 or 4 peppers)

3/4 cup heavy cream

1/2 cup grated hot pepper Jack cheese

Salt and pepper to taste

Notes:

Mustard-Basil and Red Wine Vinegarette with Pasta

Preparation

In a blender add

☐ 10 basil leaves (break or tear the leaves by hand)

☐ Minced garlic

☐ 2 cloves

☐ Pinch of kosher salt

☐ 3/4 cup red wine vinegar

Start the blender on low

☐ Slowly add 3/4 cup olive oil

☐ Add 2 tablespoons Dijon mustard

☐ Add 1 tablespoon sugar

☐ Blend until smooth

☐ Taste and adjust with salt and pepper

☐ Add a little olive oil to thicken if necessary

Ingredients

10 fresh basil leaves

Kosher salt

Crushed black pepper

Red wine vinegar

Dijon mustard

Extra virgin olive oil

Granulated sugar

3-4 garlic cloves, minced or paste form

1 pound fuseli or penne pasta

1/4 pound Asiago, Provolone or other cheese

1/2 pound dry-aged, hard or Genoa salami

1 roasted red pepper

black or green olives to taste

1/4 pound smoked turkey cold cuts

Presentation

In a large salad bowl add:

Cooked pasta (fuseli or penne)

Diced or cubed cheeses like Asiago or Provolone

Cubed pieces of salami like dry-aged, hard or Genoa

3 large slices of roasted red peppers, julienned

Pitted olives, sliced or whole, black or green

Diced or sliced pieces of smoked turkey cold cuts

Toss the above to mix then add dressing, toss again and serve

Notes:

Penne Mediterranean

Preparation

☐ Mix and cook the first 8 ingredients for 5 minutes

☐ In boiling water with salt and a little oil added, cook pasta until al dente

☐ Chop fresh parsley

Presentation

Toss and blend sauce and pasta. Add a little salt and pepper and mix. Top with Parmesan cheese and chopped parsley.

Ingredients

Extra virgin olive oil

1 large Spanish onion, chopped

16-ounce can tomato sauce

2 cloves garlic, crushed

1 cup black olives, pitted and chopped

1 tablespoon capers

Salt and black pepper to taste

1/8 teaspoon red pepper flakes

1 teaspoon cayenne pepper

1-2 cups penne pasta

Fresh parsley, chopped

Fresh Parmesan cheese, grated or shredded

Notes:

Sausage and Peppers

Preparation

☐ Slice all vegetables and set aside

☐ In a large fry pan, heat olive oil on medium heat

☐ Add whole sausages, cook until brown (about 10 minutes)

☐ Remove sausages and set aside

☐ Drain and discard juices in pan

☐ Add peppers, onion, salt and pepper to the warm fry pan and cook for 5 minutes

☐ Add oregano, dried basil leaves and garlic, stir and cook for 2 minutes

☐ Add tomatoes, wine and pepper flakes, stir and cook for 5 minutes

☐ Bring to a simmer

☐ Cut each sausage into 4-6 pieces, add to the fry pan

☐ Stir to combine and cook for 20 minutes

☐ Note: Add Balsamic vinegar at the end of cook time; stir and cook for another minute

☐ Place in a large serving bowl

☐ Add the fresh basil leaves and serve

Presentation

Serve with your choice of pasta with a marinara sauce and Parmesan cheese.

Serve fresh pineapple slices as a side dish (optional).

Wine suggestions: Chianti or Cabernet

Ingredients

2 pounds Italian sausage (1lb. sweet and 1lb. hot)

1 medium red onion, thin-sliced

2 red bell peppers, sliced in 1/2- inch slices

2 yellow bell peppers, sliced in 1/2- inch slices

2 green bell peppers, sliced in 1/2- inch slices

2 poblano peppers, sliced in 1/2- inch slices

1 tablespoon kosher salt

1 tablespoon crushed black pepper

4 cloves garlic, minced or thinly sliced

8 fresh basil leaves, sliced in a chiffenade

1 tablespoon dried oregano

1 tablespoon dried basil leaves

2 cups red wine (try Marsala wine)

28-ounce can crushed tomatoes

1/2 cup extra virgin olive oil

1 tablespoon balsamic vinegar

1 teaspoon red pepper flakes

Notes:

Spinach and Artichoke-Stuffed Shells with Ground Beef or Veal

Preparation

A. Make Filling
☐ Bring a pot of water to a boil

☐ Add frozen spinach; boil until cooked, about 15 minutes.

☐ Drain and dry spinach and reserve

☐ Drain and chop artichoke hearts and reserve

☐ Sauté onion and add ground beef or veal and brown and mix; remove, drain fat and reserve

☐ In a large mixing bowl add and mix together Spinach, Artichoke hearts, Melted butter, Basil, Oregano, Ricotta cheese, Parmesan cheese and Mozzarella cheese

B. Prepare Shells
☐ Bring a pot of water to a boil

☐ Add a little olive oil and 1 teaspoon salt

☐ Add a little olive oil and 1 teaspoon salt

☐ Add shells; return to a boil and cook uncovered

☐ Stir frequently and remove after 10-12 minutes

☐ Add shells; return to a boil and cook uncovered

☐ Stir frequently and remove after 10-12 minutes

☐ Add a little olive oil and 1 teaspoon salt

☐ Add shells; return to a boil and cook uncovered

☐ Stir frequently and remove after 10-12 minutes

☐ Drain and reserve in original pot and place lid on pot

(Continued on next page)

Ingredients

Shell Filling:
1 box large shells

15 ounces ricotta cheese

2 large eggs

2 10-ounce packages frozen chopped spinach (no sauce)

1 can artichoke hearts (8-10 count)

2 cloves garlic, minced

1 cup Parmesan cheese and have a little extra set aside for topping

2 medium sweet onions, fine chopped

1 cup mozzarella cheese and have a little extra set aside for topping

1 pound ground beef or veal

Salt and pepper to taste

2 tablespoons butter, melted

1 teaspoon dried oregano

1 teaspoon dried basil

Tomato Sauce:
4 to 6 tablespoons tomato paste

23-ounce can whole tomatoes, peeled, rough chopped, with their juice

16-ounce can tomato sauce

Salt to taste

Pepper to taste

Dried basil leaves

1 medium sweet onion, diced

2 tablespoons olive oil

2 tablespoons granulated sugar

4 cloves garlic, minced

Topping:
1 teaspoon dried oregano

1 teaspoon dried basil

Extra Parmesan cheese

Extra mozzarella cheese

Italian seasonings

C. Make Red Sauce
In a large pot add:

☐ Whole tomatoes with juices

☐ Tomato sauce

☐ Tomato paste

☐ Onion

☐ Minced garlic

☐ Granulated sugar

☐ 1/2 cup water

☐ Stir and bring to a slow boil; simmer for 20 minutes and remove

D. Fill the Shells
☐ While the red sauce is cooking, fill the shells with the filling and place on a platter or plate

E. Prepare to Bake
When red sauce is ready:

☐ Rub olive oil on bottom and sides of a large baking dish

☐ Add enough red sauce to cover bottom of baking dish

☐ Add filled shells to baking dish (place close together)

☐ Add remaining red sauce to cover shells

☐ Add some grated Parmesan and mozzarella cheese on top of covered shells

☐ Bake at 350 for 25 to 30 minutes

☐ Remove and let sit for 10 minutes before serving

☐ Sprinkle a dash of Italian seasonings on top and then ladle 3-4 shells with sauce per plate

Presentation
Serve with sliced fresh Italian bread rubbed with garlic. Serve with mixed greens salad with oil and vinegar dressing.

Wine suggestion: red zinfandel

Notes:

Vegetables

Stuffed Peppers

Preparation

☐ Cut tops off peppers, save tops

☐ Remove seeds from peppers

☐ Divide butter, brown sugar and molasses between the squash halves

☐ Bake squash at 350 degrees until soft; make sure squash is sitting in a water bath while cooking

☐ When soft, let cool and remove skins

☐ In a blender put mushrooms, onion, ground cooked turkey, cooked squash, bread crumbs and blend until mixed

☐ Stuff peppers with mixture

☐ Place pepper tops on peppers and place in baking dish

☐ Add water to cover bottom of peppers, approximately 1/3 inches deep

☐ Sprinkle olive oil on top of peppers

☐ Bake in 400 degree oven about 1 hour

Ingredients

10 mushrooms, sliced

1 pound ground turkey

1 white onion, fine chopped

1 acorn squash, cut in half, remove seeds

8 tablespoons butter

4 tablespoons brown sugar

2 tablespoons molasses

3 tablespoons bread crumbs

6 green bell peppers

Olive oil

Presentation

Serve with wild rice and pineapple slices.

Notes:

Parmesan-Cream Potatoes

Preparation

☐ Combine first 8 ingredients in a large bowl

☐ Cut potatoes into quarters, stir into sour cream mixture

☐ Arrange potatoes in a lightly greased jellyroll pan

☐ Sprinkle with Parmesan cheese

☐ Bake at 350 degrees for 50-60 minutes

Presentation

Garnish with parsley.

Ingredients

8-ounce container sour cream

1 teaspoon salt

1 teaspoon ground white pepper

1/2 teaspoon paprika

1/2 teaspoon dried thyme

1/4 teaspoon dry mustard

1/4 teaspoon hot sauce

1/4 cup butter, melted

2 1/2 pounds baking potatoes

1/4 cup Parmesan cheese, grated

Notes:

Roasted Chili Potatoes

Preparation

□ Peel and cut potatoes in half lengthwise

□ Cut potatoes into 1/4-inch-thick slices and place in a big bowl

□ Drizzle with olive oil and toss

□ Arrange potato slices in a single layer on a lightly greased cooking sheet or pan

□ Sprinkle with salt and pepper

□ Bake at 450 degrees, stirring occasionally, for 30 minutes or until golden brown

□ Combine mayonnaise, lime juice and chili powder in a large bowl

□ Add potato slices and toss

□ Spoon into serving dish

□ Sprinkle with additional chili powder

Ingredients

2 pounds baking potatoes

2 tablespoons olive oil

3/4 teaspoon salt

1/4 teaspoon pepper

1/4 cup mayonnaise

4 teaspoons fresh lime juice

1/2 teaspoon chili powder

Presentation

Garnish with parsley.

Notes:

Horseradish Mashed Potatoes

Preparation

□ Combine cream, chicken stock and horseradish in large saucepan

□ Bring to a boil, reduce heat to low and simmer until horseradish is tender, about 15 minutes

□ Meanwhile, cook potatoes in large pot with salt and water until potatoes are tender, about 20 minutes

□ Drain potatoes and return to pot

□ Add horseradish mixture to potatoes

□ Mash until smooth

Ingredients

2¾ pounds russet potatoes peeled and quartered

1 cup whipping cream

1/2 cup chicken stock

1/4 cup horseradish, peeled and grated

Parsley and chives, chopped

Presentation

Garnish with parsley and chives.

Notes:

Garlic Mashed Potatoes

Preparation

☐ Place potatoes in pot with water and a little salt, cover and bring to a boil

☐ Continue boiling until potatoes are cooked

☐ Drain water from potatoes

☐ Meanwhile, place garlic head on cookie sheet, sprinkle olive oil on garlic head, roast at 375 degrees for 15 minutes

☐ Squeeze and mince 3 cloves from roasted garlic head and add to potatoes while mashing them

☐ Add heavy cream and butter

☐ Add salt and pepper to taste

Ingredients

4 large russet potatoes, peeled and diced

1/2 pint heavy cream

1 tablespoon butter

1 garlic head

Salt and pepper to taste

Parsley and chives, chopped

Presentation

Garnish with parsley and chives. Use the remaining garlic to make a butter and garlic spread for use with a French peasant bread. Spread the garlic butter on the bread and toast the bread. Serve the bread warm with the meal or use as an appetizer by adding fresh Metal blue cheese or goat or feta cheese to the warm bread. Cut bread in triangles.

Notes:

Almond Mashed Potatoes

Preparation

□ Place potatoes in pot with water and a little salt, cover and bring to a boil

□ Continue boiling until potatoes are cooked

□ Place all of the heavy cream, 1 tablespoon almond slivers and 1 tablespoon butter in a saucepan, sauté the almond slivers for about 5 minutes

□ Strain the almond slivers, reserve the heavy cream mixture

□ Mash potatoes with the reserved heavy cream mixture

□ After mashing, mix in 1 teaspoon fresh almond slivers

□ Add salt and pepper to taste

Ingredients

4 large russet potatoes, peeled and diced

1/2 pint heavy cream

1tablespoon butter

1 tablespoon plus 1 teaspoon almond slivers

Salt and pepper to taste

Chopped parsley and chives

Presentation

Garnish with parsley and chives.

Notes:

Radar's Rice

Preparation

☐ Mix chicken stock and rice, bring to a boil

☐ Reduce heat, cover and simmer until done, about 20 minutes

☐ Add frozen peas and mix

☐ Add cheese and mix

Note: Add Worcestershire and cayenne pepper to the finished rice if you want to make Radar's Hot Rice.

Presentation

Serve with chicken or fish.

Ingredients

2 cups chicken stock or broth

1 cup frozen petite peas

2 cups long grain white rice

1/2 cup Jack or Cheddar cheese, grated

2 tablespoons Worcestershire (optional)

1 teaspoon cayenne pepper (optional)

Notes:

Spicy Rice

Preparation

☐ Sauté onion and bell pepper in olive oil over medium heat until soft

☐ Add chicken stock, stir

☐ Add Cajun spices, stir

☐ Add rice, stir and cover

☐ Cook over low heat until ready, about 20 - 25 minutes

Presentation

Serve with chicken or fish.

Ingredients

1 white onion, chopped

1 green bell pepper, chopped

2 cans chicken stock or broth

1 tablespoon Cajun spices (Emeril's Rustic Southwest or Zatarains)

2 cups long grain white rice

1 tablespoon olive oil

Notes:

Asparagus Normandie

Preparation

☐ Blanch fresh spears in boiling salt water for 6 minutes, remove spears and plunge into ice water

☐ Semi-cook or parboil bacon

☐ Wrap 1 slice of bacon around 4 asparagus spears, insert toothpick to hold bacon in place

☐ Grill asparagus wraps for 3 minutes per side

Presentation

Serve with Avignon Sauce.

For each serving stack one piece of romaine lettuce then one piece of iceberg lettuce, then a sprig of tarragon in the center of a plate. Pour sauce in the center of the place. Place asparagus on top of sauce and 5 cherry tomato halves around plate rim. Sprinkle basil on top of asparagus, followed by a little crushed black pepper and crumbled feta cheese or Maytag blue cheese. Serve with warm slices of sourdough French bread. Wine suggestions: merlot or Cabernet Sauvignon if serving steak; Pinot noir or Chardonnay if serving pork or veal.

Ingredients

Fresh asparagus spears, 4 spears per person

Bacon strips, 1 strip per 4 asparagus spears

Romaine lettuce leaves

Fresh tarragon

Cherry tomatoes, halved

fresh basil, chopped (10-12 leaves)

Feta cheese, crumbled, or Maytag blue cheese

Black pepper, crushed

Notes:

Avignon Sauce

Preparation

☐ Char-grill bell peppers

☐ Peel away charred skin, remove stem and seeds, slice into quarters

☐ Combine peppers with next four ingredients in a food processor or blender

☐ Pulse to chop ingredients

☐ Add olive oil SLOWLY while chopping, stop periodically to push ingredients into mix

☐ Toward the end of chopping, add basil

☐ Puree the mixture

Ingredients

2 red bell peppers, whole

2 or 3 shallots, rough chopped

2 garlic cloves, rough chopped

3 Roma tomatoes, seeded and quartered

1 teaspoon salt

1 teaspoon pepper

1/2 cup olive oil

2 tablespoons fresh basil, chopped

Presentation

Sauce can be served cold, warm or hot.

Notes:

Southwest Asparagus with Ham

Preparation

The tortillas:

☐ Wrap 4 asparagus spears, 2 cheese slices and 2 ham slices in tortilla

☐ Roll up tortilla, brush with olive oil and place on a cookie sheet

☐ Repeat above steps for remaining tortillas

☐ Cook at 375 degrees for 6 minutes

The sauce:

☐ Place onion, black pepper and white wine in a saucepan

☐ Bring to a boil and then simmer to reduce by half

☐ Add heavy cream and butter and whisk, continue to simmer

☐ Add lemon juice, parsley and salt

☐ Continue cooking and stirring until sauce coats the back of a spoon

Ingredients

Per serving:

 1 flour tortilla

 4 asparagus spears

 2 slices mild cheese

 2 slices ham, Prosciutto is recommended

 Olive oil

For Sauce:

 1 medium sweet onion, chopped

 Fresh black pepper

 1/2 cup white wine

 1/2 cup heavy cream

 2 sticks butter, melted

 Juice of 1 lemon

 Parsley, chopped (1/2 bunch)

 Salt to taste

Presentation

To serve, cut off ends of tortilla. Then make a straight cut 1/3 from the end for one of three pieces. Cut the remaining 2/3 tortilla diagonally and off center creating two pieces of different lengths. Stand the three pieces on their flat edges in the center of a plate forming three tiered columns. Add sauce around the tortilla columns. Add diced or sliced Roma tomatoes around the plate rim and sprinkle with chopped parsley. Wine suggestion: Chardonnay.

Notes:

Baked Mediterranean Vegetable Medley

Preparation

□ Rub a little olive oil on the bottom and sides of ramekin

□ Add layer of zucchini

□ Sprinkle with Parmesan cheese

□ Add layer of Roma tomatoes

□ Sprinkle with Parmesan cheese

□ Add layer of shallots

□ Repeat alternating layers of vegetables, cheese and shallots to near the top

□ On the final layer, add a slice or two of garden tomatoes, sprinkle bread crumbs mixed with Parmesan cheese on top

□ Add salt and pepper to taste

□ Bake at 375 degrees for 20 minutes or until done.

NOTE: place ramekin in a baking dish. Add water to baking dish to cover bottom third of ramekins, place in oven to bake.

Ingredients

1 zucchini, sliced

2 large shallots, chopped

6 Roma tomatoes, sliced

3 medium tomatoes, sliced

1/2 cup fine white bread crumbs

1/2 cup parmesan cheese, grated

Salt and pepper to taste

Olive oil

Presentation

Serve with filet mignon covered with rum and pepper glaze. Serve with herbed potatoes in sherry dressing.

Notes:

3-Potato Gratin

Preparation

☐ Rub olive oil in bottom and sides of 6 x 12 cooking dish

☐ Layer potatoes as follows:

☐ Russet, add salt and pepper

☐ Sweet potatoes, add pepper

☐ Red potatoes, add salt

☐ Repeat layers until dish is filled

☐ At the same time:

☐ Put cream, pinch of salt, 1 teaspoon pepper, garlic, butter and wine in a large saucepan

☐ Cook over medium heat, stirring occasionally, reduce by a third or half

☐ When reduced cream is ready, strain to remove garlic head, pour sauce over potatoes

☐ Top potatoes with Parmesan and mozzarella cheeses

☐ Cover with foil, bake at 375 degrees for 20 minutes

☐ Remove foil and cook uncovered 10 minutes then serve

Ingredients

2 cups heavy cream

Salt and pepper to taste

5 garlic cloves, chopped

2 tablespoons butter

1/2 cup white wine

2 sweet potatoes sliced in 1/4-inch rounds

4 red potatoes sliced in 1/4-inch rounds

2 russet or golden potatoes sliced in 1/4-inch rounds

Extra virgin olive oil

1/2 cup parmesan cheese, grated

1/2 cup mozzarella cheese, grated

Presentation

Goes well with chicken, stuffed pork chops, strip steak and white fish.

Notes:

Vegetable Medley

Preparation

□ Rub olive oil on bottom and sides of 3-inch high ramekins

□ Layer vegetables as follows:

□ Zucchini

□ Squash, sprinkle 1/2 teaspoon shallots over squash

□ Tomatoes, sprinkle 1 teaspoon Parmesan cheese over tomatoes

□ Repeat process until dish is almost full

□ Sprinkle breadcrumbs and additional Parmesan cheese on top

□ Place 1 inch of water in a baking pan, put filled ramekins in baking pan

□ Lightly cover ramekins with foil

□ Cook at 375 for 20 minutes

□ Remove foil and cook uncovered another 5-10 minutes (watch to avoid burning cheese)

□ Remove and serve

Ingredients

2 zucchini sliced in 1/8-inch round slices

2 summer squash sliced in 1/8-inch round slices

6 Roma tomatoes sliced in 1/8-inch round slices

2 medium shallots, fine diced

Salt and pepper to taste

1/2 cup fine white bread crumbs

1/2 cup parmesan cheese, grated

Extra virgin olive oil

Presentation
Goes well with chicken or filet mignon.

Notes:

3-Potato Lasagna with One-Hour Tomato Sauce

Preparation

☐ Mix tomatoes, onion, basil, parsley and oregano

☐ Add salt and pepper

☐ Rub olive oil on bottom and sides of 9 x 13 dish

☐ Layer the potatoes, adding salt, pepper, cheese and a little tomato/onion mixture between layers

☐ Repeat layering until dish is filled

☐ Pour remaining tomato mixture over top of dish and add cheese slices

☐ Cook at 375 degrees for 50 minutes or until fork tender

☐ Remove and let sit for 10 minutes

☐ Slice and serve with a topping of One-hour Tomato Sauce (page 22)

Presentation

Serve with garlic toast. Italian meatballs can also be served on the side. Wine suggestion: Chianti or Cabernet.

Ingredients

2 large sweet potatoes, peeled, cut in 1/8-inch rounds

6 red potatoes, peeled, cut in 1/8-inch rounds

2 large russet potatoes, peeled, cut in 1/8-inch rounds

4 large garden tomatoes, seeded and diced

1 large white onion, diced

8 leaves of fresh basil, fine chopped

1/4 bunch fresh parsley, fine chopped

4 leaves of fresh oregano, fine chopped

Salt and pepper to taste

Olive oil

1/2 cup Parmesan cheese, grated

1 cup Parmesan cheese, julienned

1 cup mozzarella cheese, julienned

4 garlic cloves, minced

Notes:

Sweet Potatoes Twice-Baked:

Preparation

☐ Bake whole sweet potatoes at 375 degrees for 45 minutes

☐ Remove and let sit 5 minutes

☐ Slice potatoes in half lengthwise

☐ Remove potatoes from skins and place in a mixing bowl, reserve the skins for later use

☐ Lightly mash potatoes

☐ Add honey, 1/4 cup brown sugar and 1 tablespoon butter and mash potatoes

☐ Add 1 tablespoon cinnamon and 1/2 tablespoon nutmeg and mix

☐ Spoon potato mix into potato skins

☐ Sprinkle remaining brown sugar, cinnamon and nutmeg on each potato half

☐ Add a pat of butter to each

☐ Bake at 350 degrees for 30 minutes and serve

Ingredients

4 medium sweet potatoes
1/4 cup honey
1 tablespoon nutmeg
2 tablespoons cinnamon
1/2 cup brown sugar
1/4 - 1/2 stick butter

Presentation

Goes well with chicken, pork and steak.

Notes:

Vegetable Lasagna

Preparation

☐ Saute baking sauce ingredients until soft, put in blender, blend to puree, heat again in frying pan 10 minutes.

☐ Rub olive oil on bottom and sides of a large baking dish

☐ Layer the vegetables as follows:

☐ Eggplant, sprinkle salt and pepper on top

☐ Squash, sprinkle salt and pepper on top

☐ Pour enough baking sauce mixture over squash to cover

☐ Sprinkle thyme, basil, parsley and julienned cheeses over sauce on each layer

☐ Zucchini, sprinkle salt and pepper on top

☐ Pour enough baking sauce mixture over zucchini and julienned cheeses to cover

☐ Repeat until dish is filled

☐ Place remaining julienned cheeses and grated Parmesan cheese on top

☐ Bake at 375 degrees 30-40 minutes

☐ Remove and let sit 10 minutes

☐ To serve, slice and pour some of the baking sauce over each piece

Presentation

Goes well with garlic bread or toast and a garden salad.

Ingredients

Baking Sauce:

4 garden tomatoes, peeled, seeded and diced

1 green bell pepper, seeded and diced

1 medium white onion; fine diced

3 garlic cloves, minced

Salt and pepper to taste

Oregano and basil to taste

Lasagna:

1 eggplant, sliced in 1/8-inch rounds

2 zucchini, sliced in 1/8-inch rounds

1 white onion, sliced in 1/8-inch rounds

4 sprigs fresh thyme, chopped

8 fresh basil leaves, chopped

1/2 bunch fresh parsley, chopped

1 cup Parmesan cheese, julienned

1 cup mozzarella cheese, julienned

1/2 cup Parmesan cheese, grated

Extra virgin olive oil

Notes:

Mixed-Vegetable Stir-Fry

Preparation

☐ Heat oil in large skillet over medium-high heat 2 minutes

☐ Add garlic and next 3 ingredients, stir-fry 2 minutes

☐ Add onion and next 3 ingredients, stir-fry 5 minutes

☐ Add broccoli and mushrooms, stir-fry 3 minutes

☐ Stir in basil and sherry, stir-fry 4 minutes or until carrots are crisp tender

Presentation

Wine suggestion: chilled white zinfandel or buttery Chardonnay.

Note: To make a pork stir-fry:

☐ Cut 12 ounces of lean, boneless pork loin chops into thin strips

☐ Heat oil in a large skillet over medium-high heat 2 minutes

☐ Add pork and stir-fry 6 minutes

☐ Add garlic and next 3 ingredients and proceed as directed above

Wine suggestion: red Zinfandel

Ingredients

2 teaspoons hot pepper oil

2 garlic cloves, minced

2 carrots, thinly sliced

2 celery ribs, thinly sliced

3 tablespoons hoisin sauce

1 large sweet onion, cut in half and thinly sliced

1 large green bell pepper, julienned

1 small zucchini, sliced

1 small yellow squash, sliced

1 cup fresh broccoli florets

8-ounce package mushrooms, sliced

1 tablespoon fresh basil, chopped

2 tablespoons sherry

Notes:

Sandwiches

Mediterranean Muffalato

Preparation

The Dressing:
☐ In a medium-size bowl, mix vinegar, olive oil, basil, salt and pepper

The Filling:
☐ In a large bowl, mix olives, onion, tomatoes, Parmesan and mozzarella cheeses, garlic and a pinch of salt and pepper

☐ Pour dressing over filling, mix thoroughly

The Kaiser Roll:
☐ Cut the top out of each roll about the size of a silver dollar, save the top for a lid

☐ Remove some of the bread inside the roll, making a hollow center

☐ Spoon filling into each roll, cover with lid

☐ Wrap rolls in aluminum foil and place on a cookie sheet

☐ Bake at 350 degrees, 25-30 minutes

☐ Remove from oven, wrap each foil packet in a colorful napkin

Ingredients

2 teaspoons dried basil

1 teaspoon kosher salt

1 teaspoon crushed black pepper

1/4 cup red wine vinegar

1 cup Kalamata olives, pitted and diced

1/4 cup extra virgin olive oil

1 medium Spanish or Vidalia onion, diced

2 garlic cloves, minced

4 Roma tomatoes, rough chopped

1 cup Parmesan cheese, grated

1 cup fresh mozzarella cheese, cut and diced

4-6 Kaiser rolls

Presentation

Serve warm. Wine suggestion: chilled red zinfandel or Pinot grigio.

Notes:

Sauerkraut with Bratwurst – On the Grill

Preparation

☐ Melt butter in 4 quart pot over medium heat

☐ Add onion, pepper, bay leaves, garlic, sauerkraut and beer, mix

☐ Bring to a boil, then simmer for 5 minutes

☐ Place sauerkraut mixture in a casserole dish and bake uncovered at 375 degrees for 20 minutes

☐ Mix sour cream, dijonaise and horseradish in a bowl, refrigerate until ready to use

☐ Grill hot dogs, bratwursts, polish dogs, etc.

☐ Serve grilled meat in buns topped with sauerkraut and sour cream mixture

Ingredients

2 tablespoons butter

1 large sweet onion, sliced

Pepper to taste

3 bay leaves

1 garlic clove, minced

2 pounds sauerkraut, drained

1 bottle of beer

3/4 cup sour cream

1/4 cup dijonaise

1/4 cup fresh horseradish

Hot dogs, bratwursts, polish dogs, etc.

Presentation

Serve with baked potatoes that have been rubbed in olive oil and sprinkled with herbs and spices to taste.

Notes

Apple-Bacon Burgers

Preparation

□ Sauté onion, apple, and 1/4 teaspoon sage in a skillet in hot oil over medium heat for 3 minutes, set aside

□ Combine ground beef, 1/4 teaspoon sage, Worcestershire sauce, salt and pepper in a bowl, shape into 12 patties

□ Top 6 patties with apple mixture

□ Place remaining 6 patties on top of prepared patties, press edges to seal, making 6 large burgers

□ Wrap edges of each burger with 2 bacon slices, insert toothpick to hold bacon in place

□ Place burgers on broiler pan

□ Broil for 10 minutes per side; keep meat 5 inches away from heat

Ingredients

1 small yellow onion, chopped

1 Granny Smith apple, chopped

1/2 teaspoon ground sage

1 teaspoon olive oil

2 pounds lean ground beef

3 tablespoons white wine

3 tablespoons Worcestershire sauce

1 teaspoon kosher salt

1/2 teaspoon pepper

12 bacon slices

6 sesame seed buns, toasted

Presentation

Serve with desired toppings. Remember to remove toothpicks from burgers!

Notes:

Inside Out Cheeseburger

Preparation

☐ Combine first 4 ingredients in a large bowl

☐ Shape into 12 patties, set aside

☐ Sauté onion slices in a non-stick skillet coated with cooking spray for 10 minutes or until tender

☐ Top 6 patties with onion, cheese and relish

☐ Place remaining 6 patties on top of prepared patties, press edges to seal, making 6 large burgers

☐ Cook burgers 3 at a time in non-stick skillet over medium heat for 8 minutes per side or until beef is no longer pink

☐ Remove and keep warm on a plate in oven (200 degrees) until ready to serve

☐ Toast buns in skillet

Ingredients

2 pounds lean ground beef

1½ teaspoons kosher salt

3/4 teaspoon pepper

1/4 cup Dijon mustard

6, 1/2-inch thick slices red onion

6, 1-ounce sharp Cheddar cheese slices

1/2 cup pickle relish

6 large sesame seed buns, toasted

Toppings: mayonnaise, mustard, leaf lettuce, tomato slices

Presentation

Serve with desired toppings.

Notes:

Stuffed Southwestern-Style Burgers

Preparation

☐ Mash avocado with a fork in a small bowl

☐ Stir in plum tomatoes, garlic, lemon juice, 1/2 teaspoon salt and 1/2 teaspoon pepper, set aside

☐ Combine beef, onion, 1 teaspoon salt, 1 teaspoon pepper and chili powder

☐ Shape into 12 patties

☐ Top 6 patties with cheese cubes and avocado mix

☐ Place remaining 6 patties on top of prepared patties, press edges to seal, making 6 large burgers

☐ Place burgers on a broiler pan and broil for 10 minutes on each side or until beef is no longer pink

☐ Remove from oven and let rest for 2 minutes

☐ Toast buns and serve

Presentation

Serve with desired toppings.

Ingredients

1 avocado

3 plum tomatoes, chopped

1 garlic clove, minced

2 teaspoons lemon juice

1½ teaspoons salt

1½ teaspoons pepper

2 pounds lean ground beef

1 small yellow onion, diced

2 teaspoons chili powder

8-ounce package Monterey Jack cheese with peppers, cubed

6 large sesame seed buns, toasted

Toppings: leaf lettuce, tomato slices, red onion slices

Notes:

Mushroom-Stuffed Hamburger Steaks

Preparation

☐ Melt butter or margarine in large skillet

☐ Add onion and mushrooms, sauté over medium heat for 3 minutes or until tender, remove from skillet

☐ Combine beef and next 7 ingredients in a large bowl

☐ Shape into 8 patties

☐ Top 4 patties with onion mixture

☐ Place remaining 4 patties on top of prepared patties, press edges to seal, making 4 large burgers

☐ Wrap edges of each burger with 2 bacon slices, insert toothpick to hold bacon in place

☐ Place burgers on a rack and put the rack in a broiler pan

☐ Broil for 10 minutes per side; keep meat 5½ inches away from heat

Presentation

Serve with desired toppings. Remember to remove toothpicks from burgers!

Ingredients

1 tablespoon butter or margarine

1 small yellow onion, chopped

6 fresh mushrooms, sliced

2 pounds lean ground beef

1/2 medium russet or golden potato, shredded

1 large egg, lightly beaten

1/4 cup ketchup

1 tablespoon all-purpose flour

1 tablespoon Worcestershire sauce

1/2 teaspoon kosher salt

1/2 teaspoon pepper

8 bacon slices

Notes:

Breakfast

Tomato-Basil Frittata

Preparation

☐ Cook onion slices slowly over low heat in olive oil in large fry pan

☐ Add tomatoes and a little salt and pepper, cook 10 minutes, stirring occasionally

☐ Remove onions and tomatoes from the pan and let cool

☐ Beat eggs until well mixed

☐ Place onions and tomatoes back in fry pan

☐ Add eggs and a little more salt and pepper

☐ Add Parmesan cheese and mix

☐ Add basil and stir

☐ Cook over low heat 15 minutes until the eggs set, leave the top runny (do not stir during cooking time)

☐ Place fry pan under broiler 1-2 minutes

☐ Remove, let cool a little and cut into "V" shaped wedges for serving

Ingredients

3 medium Spanish onions, thinly sliced

Kosher salt and crushed black pepper to taste

4 tablespoons olive oil

1 large can plum tomatoes, drained and chopped

6 large eggs

3 tablespoons Parmesan cheese, grated

8 fresh basil leaves, rough chopped, or 2 teaspoons dried basil leaves

Olive oil

Presentation

Serve with a pineapple slice.

Notes:

The Breakfast Club

Preparation

☐ Spread Creole mustard on one slice of bread

☐ Add a layer of arugula or spinach, followed by the fried egg and roasted red pepper

☐ Spread Creole mustard on a second slice of bread

☐ Add a sausage patty and shredded cheeses

☐ Place the second slice of bread in a toaster oven or under a broiler to melt cheeses

☐ Place second slice on top of the first slice

☐ Place the third slice on top of the second slice

☐ Cut sandwich in an "X" shape to make wedges

Ingredients

1 fried egg with a hard yolk

1 sausage patty

Shredded mixed cheeses such as Provolone, Gruyère and Cheddar

Tomato slices (optional)

1 roasted red pepper per sandwich

Arugula or baby spinach leaves

Creole mustard

3 slices of bread, toasted

Presentation

Serve with a bowl of fresh fruit. Serve with a plate of tomato slices on a bed of spinach leaves. Serve with water, coffee or a Mimosa.

Notes:

Pecan French Toast

Preparation

☐ Blend eggs with half and half, sugar, vanilla, nutmeg, cinnamon, ginger and Allspice

☐ Add pecans and half of orange zest to batter

☐ Heat butter in non-stick fry pan over medium heat

☐ Dip bread slices in batter, remove excess batter

☐ Place bread in pan, cook slowly over low heat for 2 minutes per side

Presentation

Serve with fresh berries and powdered sugar. Add long strips of orange zest on top of bread slices, serve warm syrup on the side.

Ingredients

5 eggs, whisked

1 ½ cups half and half

2 tablespoons granulated sugar

1/2 teaspoon vanilla

1/2 teaspoon nutmeg

2 teaspoons cinnamon

1/2 teaspoon ginger

1/2 teaspoon Allspice

1/2 cup ground pecans

Zest of one orange

1 tablespoon butter

French peasant bread, sliced into 1/2-inch thick slices

Powdered sugar

Blueberries or strawberries

Maple syrup

Notes:

Cajun Frittata with Tomatoes and Chorizo

Preparation

☐ Heat oil in fry pan over high heat

☐ Sauté celery, pepper and onion, set aside when done

☐ Add sausage to pan, cook until brown, drain the grease from the pan, set aside

☐ Add onions to pan, sauté until light brown

☐ Add chopped tomatoes, salt and pepper

☐ Cook 10 minutes, stirring occasionally, set aside and reserve until cool

☐ In a large bowl beat eggs until well-mixed but not frothy (add a little milk)

☐ Add cooled vegetables, Parmesan cheese, sausage, and celery, pepper and onion mixture

☐ Add grated cheeses and ground fresh pepper, stir

☐ Add basil, stir

☐ Melt butter in a 12-inch non-stick fry pan over high heat

☐ Pour in egg mixture

☐ Reduce heat to low and cook 15 minutes until eggs are set but the top is still a bit runny

☐ Place pan in the oven under the broiler for 30-60 seconds

☐ Check pan to see if frittata is ready: the frittata should be firm and have pulled away from the sides of the pan

☐ Remove from oven, loosen with a spatula and slide onto a large serving dish (it should slide easily and look like a pizza)

☐ Cut in wedges and serve

Ingredients

3 medium onions, thinly sliced

4 tablespoons olive oil

1 large can whole plum tomatoes with basil, drained

Salt and pepper to taste

6 large eggs

6 tablespoons Parmesan cheese, grated

1/4 cup grated Cheddar and pepper Jack cheeses, grated

10 fresh basil leaves, torn or chopped into smaller pieces

4 tablespoons butter

4-6 hot sausages (chorizo, Cajun or Mexican) ground or thin sliced

1/2 cup celery, diced

1/2 cup green pepper, diced

1/4 cup onion, diced

Presentation

Serve warm or cold hash browns or home fries and garlic toast.

Notes

123

Potato, Red Onion and Goat Cheese Frittata

Preparation

□ Fill small pot two-thirds full with water, bring to a boil

□ Add salt and potatoes, cook until tender, 18-20 minutes

□ Drain potatoes, cool 12-15 minutes, cut into I-inch cubes

□ Pre-heat oven to 375 degrees

□ Warm olive oil over medium heat in a10-inch ovenproof pan

□ Add onion and sauté, stirring occasionally, until tender (5-6 minutes)

□ Add potatoes, garlic and basil, sauté and stir for 1-2 minutes

□ Add eggs, salt, pepper and cheese, stir until just mixed

□ Place pan in oven and bake until frittata is set, about 18-20 minutes

Ingredients

Salt and pepper to taste

3 medium new potatoes

2 teaspoons olive oil

1 small red onion, peeled and cut into I-inch wedges

Pinch of chopped garlic

8-10 basil leaves, sliced or slivered

6 eggs, lightly beaten

4 ounces goat cheese (Chèvre), broken into 1/2-inch chunks

Presentation

Serves 4. For breakfast, serve with various sausages and toasted 7-grain bread with garlic butter spread. For lunch, cut into pie-slice pieces and serve with garden salad with honey mustard dressing and garnished with mandarin orange slices.
Wine suggestion: chilled Chardonnay.

For dinner, serve with flank steak and vegetable medley.
Wine suggestion: Merlot.

Notes:

Desserts

Pineapple Honeycomb

Preparation

☐ Remove pineapple's skin.

☐ Remove pineapple's hard center (optional).

☐ Mix cinnamon, sugar and nutmeg.

☐ Dry rub cinnamon, sugar and nutmeg all over pineapple.

☐ Pour one cup of honey over pineapple.

☐ Mix brown sugar and crushed nuts.

☐ Rub brown sugar and nuts all over pineapple.

☐ Pour more honey if needed over the pineapple to help hold the nuts in place.

☐ Refrigerate for several hours.

☐ When ready to serve, remove from refrigerator and cut into slices.

☐ Scoop some of the sauce into the center hole of each pineapple slice or, if no hole, scoop it onto the center of the slice.

Ingredients

1 fresh and ripe pineapple, whole

1/4 cup cinnamon

2 tablespoons granulated sugar

1 cup brown sugar

2 tablespoons nutmeg

1 cup walnuts or pecans, dried, toasted and crushed or chopped

1-2 cups honey

Presentation

Serve as dessert with pork entree.

It's a little messy but tastes great!

Notes:

Hot Spiced Fruit

Preparation

☐ Drain fruits and place in shallow 2-quart baking dish.

☐ Sprinkle with brown sugar, curry powder, cinnamon and nutmeg.

☐ Slice butter or margarine over fruit. Bake at 350 for 45-50 minutes.

Presentation

Makes 6 to 8 servings.

Ingredients

1, 16-ounce can sliced peaches

1, 16-ounce can pear halves

1, 16-ounce can pineapple chunks

1, 17-ounce can figs

8 Maraschino cherries

1 tablespoon packed brown sugar

1 teaspoon curry powder

1 teaspoon cinnamon

1/2 teaspoon nutmeg

2 tablespoons butter or margarine

Notes:

Tangerine Flambé

Preparation

c Melt 4 tablespoons of butter in frying pan.

□ Add tangerine juice.

□ Add 6-8 tangerines.

□ Add a pinch of nutmeg and cinnamon.

□ Add 1/4 cup sugar.

□ Add tangerine zest.

□ Add heavy cream at the end of Basting/cooking for 1 minute

□ Add 2 more tablespoons of butter, then add 1/4 cup Grand Marnier.

□ Remove from heat and ignite the Grand Marnier.

□ Flambé the tangerines and serve.

Ingredients

6-8 tangerines, peeled, whole

Nutmeg

Cinnamon

6 tablespoons of butter

1/4 cup sugar

Juice of 1 tangerine

Zest of 1 tangerine

1/2 pint heavy cream

Grand Marnier

Presentation

Serve 2 tangerines per plate. On each plate add a little sauce, sprinkle with a little zest and add a little nutmeg. Top with vanilla ice cream and a drizzle of Grand Marnier.

Notes:

Almond-Lemonade Tea

Preparation

□ Stir all ingredients together in a large pitcher until sugar dissolves.

Presentation

Serve over ice.

Ingredients

4 cups brewed tea, chilled

3 cups cold water

6-ounce can frozen lemonade concentrate, thawed

1/4 cup granulated sugar

1 teaspoon almond extract

Raspberry Spritzer

Preparation

□ Put raspberries in a blender, process until smooth, then strain

□ Combine raspberry puree and concentrates in a 2 gallon container.

□ Add ice and chill for 30 minutes.

□ Stir in ginger ale just before serving.

Presentation

Optional: mix white wine with cocktail. Serve with a mint sprig and a lemon or lime wedge.

Ingredients

1, 10-ounce package frozen raspberries, thawed

1, 12-ounce can frozen cranberry juice concentrate, thawed

1, 12-ounce can frozen pink lemonade concentrate, thawed

2, 2-liter bottles of ginger ale, chilled

Fresh mint sprigs

Lemon or lime wedges

Notes:

129

The Breeze

Preparation

☐ In a large sauce pan, bring 1 quart of water to a boil.

☐ Add 1 cup sugar and keep boiling.

☐ Add 1 cup each blueberries, strawberries and raspberries.

☐ Keep boiling and stirring as the berries reduce to form a syrup.

☐ Add 1/4 cup Grand Marnier. Keep stirring and boiling.

☐ When consistency is syrupy remove from heat.

☐ Pour mixture into a 2-inch high, 6- by 9-inch pan, cover with foil and place in freezer for a minimum of 2 hours.

☐ Remove from freezer and slice into 1-inch wide by 6-inch long slices.

Ingredients

1 cup granulated sugar

1 package each fresh blueberries, strawberries and raspberries

Grand Marnier

Champagne

Presentation

Place a berry slice in a Champagne glass and add Champagne when serving.

Notes:

A Berry Surprise

Preparation

c Mix package of berries and 1/2 cup sugar in a bowl.

c Put 1 cup of sugared berries in a blender, add 1/2 cup port wine and puree the mixture.

□ Pour puree over remaining berries in the bowl.

□ Refrigerate a minimum of 2 hours.

Ingredients

1 package mixed berries
1/2 cup granulated sugar
Port wine
Short cake or biscuits
Ice cream or yogurt
Grand Marnier

Presentation

Serve with short cake or biscuits. Place ice cream or yogurt on short cake or biscuit, ladle berry mixture on top. Drizzle Grand Marnier over berries.

Notes:

Mango Margarita

Preparation

☐ Puree mango, ice, tequila, powdered sugar, triple sec and lime juice in blender until smooth.

Presentation

Serve in Margarita glasses. Serves 4.

Ingredients

2 large mangoes, peeled and chopped

2½ cups ice cubes

6 tablespoons gold tequila

6 tablespoons powdered sugar

3 tablespoons triple sec or orange liqueur

2 tablespoons fresh lime juice

Banana Supreme

Preparation

☐ Place 4 whole, peeled bananas in a Corning dish.

☐ Add brown sugar to coat bananas liberally. Add raisins and nuts.

☐ Bake at 350 for 5 minutes.

☐ Remove from oven and add jigger of light rum and jigger of dark rum to the bananas.

☐ Toss and mix the bananas and rum then serve.

Presentation

Serve with ice cream or sherbet. Top with shredded coconut.

Ingredients

4 whole bananas

4 tablespoons brown sugar

1/4 cup raisins–brown and yellow mixed

1/4 cup sliced almonds or crushed walnuts or pecans

Shredded fresh coconut

Light and dark rum

Vanilla ice cream or orange sherbet

Notes:

LaVergne, TN USA
20 January 2011
213276LV00004B/2/P